COMING EVENTS IN PROPHECY

COMING EVENTS IN PROPHECY

M. R. DeHAAN, M.D.

ZONDERVAN
PUBLISHING HOUSE   OF THE ZONDERVAN CORPORATION
GRAND RAPIDS, MICHIGAN 49506

COMING EVENTS IN PROPHECY
Copyright 1962 by
Radio Bible Class
Grand Rapids, Michigan

Copyright assigned to M. R. DeHaan, 1966

Twentieth printing August 1980
ISBN 0-310-23301-1

Printed in the United States of America

FOREWORD

It is a signal honor for me to be permitted a Foreword to this latest volume from the gifted pen of one of the truly great living expositors of the Word of God, my dearly beloved brother in the Lord, Dr. Martin R. DeHaan. Reading the manuscript has been a heart-warming and soul-challenging experience. Fully documented with Scripture, this book has clarity, depth, and a moving quality which not only stimulates the mind, but also makes an appeal to the heart. Personally, I am deeply grateful to Dr. DeHaan for taking time out of his extraordinary radio and pulpit ministry to make another fine contribution to first-class, fundamental Christian literature. He has done the Church of Christ immeasurable service by putting into print the results of his long and prayerful study of the vital subject of the return of the Lord. Thus his vigorous Bible teachings are preserved for years to come.

I am fully in accord with Dr. DeHaan's statement: "Ignorance of God's prophetic outline, failure to know God's program for the Church, the nations, and Israel, is the cause of the overwhelming amount of error and misunderstanding of the events of the future." Certainly in all the years that I have been teaching and preaching the prophetic Scriptures, I have never witnessed such confusion within and without the Church. There are very few who, like Dr. DeHaan, are sufficiently acquainted with the prophetic Word to present it accurately, and thereby to attempt to bring order out of the chaos that exists in the minds of men today. I have the conviction that never has any book been published more applicable to "a time like this," and I wish for it the widest circulation under the blessing of God.

It has been a delight to follow the author as he brings Scriptural proofs to bear upon the teaching of the Second Coming of Christ from the first promise given from Heaven after the ascension of the Lord Jesus, in Acts 1:11, to the last promise from Christ Himself in Revelation 22:20. Dr. DeHaan deals definitely and clearly with the eight last events of the end time. He stresses the place accorded to the Lord's return in the writings of Paul, John, James, Peter, and Jude. The passages in this book which show the emphasis the Bible puts upon

Foreword

the imminence of the return of our Lord are stirring indeed and greatly needed at this particular time. I feel that this blessed aspect of the Second Coming has been almost lost in the argumentation and frustrations that plague the churches of the present day. The majority of the Lord's people are not, like the Thessalonians, daily "waiting for His Son from Heaven." Thoroughly, but briefly, the teaching of the Rapture, the Tribulation, and the Millennium, with related truths, is covered, and with kindness and frankness some disordered views are corrected.

It was refreshing to me to note how justly Dr. DeHaan deals with the Word of God. Without equivocation or exaggeration, without an attempt to force his own interpretation, he allows the Bible to speak for itself. It is my heart's desire that this volume may be placed in the hands of thousands of pastors, missionaries, and Christian workers, and that particularly it may reach young ministers who are wavering in their views of these vital prophetic truths. It is appalling that the Church of this generation should be deprived of their heritage, especially in view of II Peter 1:19 — "We have also a more sure word of prophecy; whereunto ye do well that ye take heed, as unto a light that shineth in a dark place, until the day dawn, and the day star arise in your hearts." A return to the prophetic Scriptures, and an impartation of them to longing hearts in the churches, will add a spark and a vitality that has not been seen for many a day, and will strengthen the faith of God's people in dark days.

I feel confident that Dr. DeHaan's prayer that "These chapters will help in a better understanding of the program of God for this world, and cause people to rightly divide the Word and intelligently 'discern the signs of the times'" will be answered abundantly. I can assure him that I will join him in this request at the throne of grace.

LOUIS T. TALBOT, D.D.
Chancellor of the Bible Institute of Los Angeles

INTRODUCTION

More than nineteen hundred years ago the angels announced the birth of Jesus with the promise, "On earth peace, good will toward men" (Luke 2:14). The centuries have come and gone and yet there is no peace among the nations, and good will among men sounds like idle mockery amid the clanging of tanks, the roar of airplanes, and explosions of nuclear bombs. That promise is as yet unfulfilled. Nineteen hundred years ago Jesus taught His disciples to pray, "Thy kingdom come. Thy will be done in earth, as it is in heaven" (Matthew 6:10). That prayer has remained unanswered for almost two millenniums and we seem farther removed from its realization than ever before. More than nineteen hundred years ago the first message Jesus sent from Heaven after His ascension on the Mount of Olives was, "This same Jesus, which is taken up from you into heaven, shall so come in like manner as ye have seen him go into heaven" (Acts 1:11). That promise has never yet been fulfilled. More than nineteen hundred years ago the Holy Spirit closed the canon of Scripture with the last promise of our ascended Saviour, "Surely I come quickly. Amen" (Revelation 22:20a). The last word of Jesus awaits fulfillment after almost two millenniums. The last prayer of the Bible, "Even so, come, Lord Jesus" (Revelation 22:20b) has been greeted by silence for all these years. Either these promises did not mean what they said, or they must still lie in the future.

All evangelicals believe that these promises will be fulfilled to the letter. There is nothing more certain than the return of the Lord Jesus. The uncertainty lies in the TIME and not in the FACT. Time means nothing with God. He is the timeless one and with Him one day is "as a thousand years, and a thousand years as one day" (II Peter 3:8). Two thousand years or more are with God only a "little while." The writer of Hebrews says: "For yet a *little while*, and he that shall come will come, and will not tarry" (Hebrews 10:37).

That was over nineteen hundred years ago, and yet that "little while" has not yet passed. But He will come, and here is a sobering thought, even though it sounds simple and platitudinous — we are now nineteen hundred years *nearer* the fulfillment of all these promises than when they were first spoken. Yes, the promise of the angels, "peace on earth," will some day be realized; the prayer, "Thy kingdom come," will be answered; the promise, "this same Jesus . . . shall so come," will be kept to the letter. And the last prayer of the Bible, "Even so, come, Lord Jesus," will be uttered for the last time when, ". . . the Lord himself shall descend from heaven with a shout . . ." (I Thessalonians 4:16).

All evangelical Christians believe this, but they are by no means agreed about the details. The enemy has been quick to take advantage of the conflict of interpretations among evangelicals and has introduced all sorts of false and fantastic interpretations. Deception has been on the increase. Jesus, however, mentioned in Matthew 24:14 that one of the first signs of the end of the age would be *deception*. He said: ". . . Take heed that no man deceive you" (Matthew 24:4).

This same warning is repeated again in Mark 13:5 and in Luke 21:8. The "end of the age" and the last days would be characterized as days of "deception." Surely there is no precedent in history for the present day, with its deceptions, cults, sects, and isms, and about which Jesus said that false christs and false prophets would arise, and ". . . shew signs and wonders, to seduce, if it were possible, even the elect" (Mark 13:22).

This confusion has invaded even the ranks of the fundamentalists, and here too we find error and misunderstanding. We have the pre-millennial, the post-millennial and the a-millennial schools. And even among the "pre's" we have utter confusion, some saying this and others that. We have the pre-tribulationists, the post-tribulation pre-millennialists, the mid-tribulationists and the partial rapturists, etc. This confusion of tongues among Christians is in itself a sign of the last days, for Jesus predicted that these days would be characterized by "deception," and places this warning at the head of all the signs in Matthew, Mark, and Luke.

The confusion is not limited to believers, however, but characterizes above all, the condition in the world. Millions are deceived by the glowing promises of communism. Other millions are deceived into believing that democracy is the answer to man's problems. Other millions, yea, most people in the world still dream of an age of peace and prosperity by the efforts of man, by conference, integration, legislation, and a United Nations. Other millions are deceived into believing that religious ecumenicism will bring in the golden age of a future Utopia. In the words of David, God laughs at all these human attempts to solve his problems by his own wisdom. But after millenniums of wars, strife, struggle, and suffering, after all man's progress in the field of education, technology, travel, and advance in every realm of industry, science, space travel, and nuclear discovery, the world is in a worse mess than ever before in all history, and the words of Jesus crash upon us like a clap of thunder: ". . . signs in the sun, and in the moon, and in the stars; and *upon earth distress of nations, with perplexity* . . ." (Luke 21:25).

In the firm, unshakable conviction that man, if left alone, will soon bring about his own complete destruction, we assert that the only hope for this old world is the *Second Coming of Jesus Christ.* There is no other answer — no other solution, and this is just what the Bible says. There is not one verse in the Bible which tells us to *look for, wait for, or watch for,* anything, as a final solution to the world's problems *except the return of the Lord.*

This firm conviction is, therefore, the reason for the publishing of this volume, *Coming Events in Prophecy.* Because we believe the coming of the Lord draweth near, because we believe it is the world's only hope, we are sending out these messages with the prayer that these chapters will help in a better understanding of the program of God for this world, and cause people to *rightly divide the Word* and intelligently "discern the signs of the times" (Matthew 16:3).

Much of the confusion among believers is due to plain ignorance concerning prophecy. Thousands of believers, including ministers and preachers, avoid the study of prophecy because of the confusion which exists, but they have the horse behind the cart — the confusion is the result of *neglecting* the study of prophecy. Not one in a hundred of the members of our evangelical churches could give the order of events of the last days, and hence do not know what to look for. Ignorance of God's prophetic outline, failure to know God's program for the Church, the nations, and Israel, is the cause of the overwhelming amount of error and misunderstanding of the events of the future. It is in the hope of stimulating a desire for deeper personal study, that the simple outline studies in this volume are sent out. We believe the Bible has the answer to all present-day world problems, and until we can fit current events and the international situation into the program of God, we must continue in confusion and grope blindly about in a fog of uncertainty and fear. We believe that, using the outline of events in the following chapters as a framework and skeleton, you will by earnest study be able to fit whatever happens into its proper place in the program of God, and with the clear outline of prophecy you will be able to appreciate the words of Jesus: "And when these things *begin* to come to pass, then *look up,* and *lift up your heads;* for your redemption draweth nigh" (Luke 21:28).

C O N T E N T S

Foreword

Introduction

Chapter One

THE UNANSWERED PRAYER

For more than nineteen hundred years Christians have been repeating the prayer which Jesus taught His disciples, "Thy kingdom come. Thy will be done in earth, as it is in heaven" (Matthew 6:10).

This prayer has never been answered, for we cannot say, even by the widest stretch of the imagination or the extremest method of spiritualizing this petition, that peace on earth has come, or that God's will is being done on earth as it is in Heaven. On the contrary, war has been on the increase, and rebellion and violence against God has never been as intense as it is today. And yet that prayer is going to be fully answered some day, and we are nearer that day than ever before. The prayer, "Thy kingdom come," when His will shall "be done on earth as it is in heaven," will yet be fulfilled. All indications point to the soon return of the King. Believing as we do that there is no hope for this floundering, blundering old world in this atomic age through the efforts of man, we turn to the Word of God for an answer, and find that God has a program, and a plan which is running exactly on time. Only as we turn to this infallible Book, the Bible, can we know what lies ahead, and its predictions are infallible. Every single prophesied event fulfilled in the past, has been literally fulfilled without fail just exactly as the Bible said it would be. Since all fulfilled prophecies have been absolutely reliable, we can with confidence accept all the remaining prophecies of the future with equal certainty. The fulfilled prophecies were brought to pass *literally*, and therefore the unfulfilled prophecies will be consummated with the same literalness. We turn therefore to the infallible Word of God for an answer to man's question, "What lies ahead in this atomic age?"

One of the first essentials in the understanding of the program of God for the future is to know the teaching of the Scrip-

15

tures concerning the chronological sequence and steps in these last days ending in the fulfillment of the unanswered prayer Jesus taught His disciples, "Thy kingdom come." Fix clearly in your mind the several successive steps in the completion of God's program, and it will greatly help you in the enjoyment of all that follows.

We shall mention eight things which the Bible says must still happen before earth's history comes to a final close. The first one of these eight momentous future events in world history may occur at any moment, for it is an undated event. We begin therefore with EVENT NUMBER ONE! It is the personal return of the Lord Jesus Christ from Heaven according to His promise. The same Jesus who lived and died and rose and ascended into Heaven more than nineteen hundred years ago is coming again. He Himself said so. He said, "I will come again" (John 14:3). The first promise He sent back from Heaven after His ascension was by the angels who said "this same Jesus is coming back" (Acts 1:11), and the last promise in the Bible is "Surely I come quickly" (Revelation 22:20).

The Apostle Paul says in I Thessalonians 4:

> . . . The Lord himself shall descend from heaven with a shout, with the voice of the archangel, and with the trump of God: and the dead in Christ shall rise first:
>
> Then we which are alive and remain shall be caught up together with them in the clouds, to meet the Lord in the air: and so shall we ever be with the Lord (I Thessalonians 4:16, 17).

This then we believe is the next event on God's calendar. It is a future event which, however, may happen any moment. All believers (the dead raised, the living changed) will be taken *up out of this world,* to meet the Lord *in the air.* This event, Number One, we call the Translation of the Church.

EVENT NUMBER TWO will follow immediately. It is called in the Bible *the Day of the Lord,* the day of Jacob's trouble, God's day of wrath, and still better known as the Tribulation. It will be a brief, intense period of the greatest tribulation and sorrow the world has ever known in all of its history. Jesus describes it as follows: "For then shall be great tribulation, such as was not since the beginning of the world to this time, no, nor ever shall be" (Matthew 24:21).

It will be a time of war, destruction, violence, bloodshed, and terror without precedent, with great judgment let loose upon the earth, a time so terrible that only the intervention of God will prevent man from utterly destroying himself. Of this day Jesus said: "And except those days should be shortened, there should no flesh be saved . . ." (Matthew 24:22).

This second event — the Tribulation — will culminate in EVENT NUMBER THREE. The Battle of Armageddon will conclude the Great Tribulation, when all the nations of the world will be gathered for battle in the Middle East, and will be crushed and defeated when they invade the Land of Palestine and attack the city of Jerusalem. This final battle at the close of the Tribulation, and described in many passages of Scripture, and epitomized in Revelation, chapters 6 to 19, will be terminated suddenly by the public appearance of the Lord Jesus Christ with His armies of saints, descending from Heaven to the Mount of Olives, and utterly destroying the armies of Satan. This is EVENT NUMBER FOUR, the public return of Jesus Christ, to put an end to man's rebellion. It is described:

> And I saw heaven opened, and behold a white horse; and he that sat upon him was called Faithful and True. . . .
> And the armies which were in heaven followed him. . . .
> And he hath on his vesture and on his thigh a name written, KING OF KINGS, AND LORD OF LORDS (Revelation 19:11, 14, 16).

Of this event Zechariah says:

> Then shall the LORD go forth, and fight against those nations. . . .
> And his feet shall stand in that day upon the mount of Olives. . . .
> And the LORD shall be king over all the earth: in that day shall there be one LORD, and his name one (Zechariah 14:3, 4, 9).

This is the Second Coming, or coming of the Lord, and is to be distinguished from the Translation of the Church, in which the Church meets the Lord in the air before the Tribulation. But at the Second Coming, the Lord comes to the earth Himself, His feet standing upon the Mount of Olives. It comes therefore at the close of the Tribulation. Jesus Himself said:

> Immediately after the tribulation of those days shall the sun be darkened, and the moon shall not give her light, and the stars shall fall from heaven, and the powers of the heavens shall be shaken:
> And then shall appear the sign of the Son of man in

heaven: and then shall all the tribes of the earth mourn, and they shall see the Son of man coming in the clouds of heaven with power and great glory (Matthew 24:29, 30).

We are now ready for the next event, EVENT NUMBER FIVE. It is the establishment of the Messianic Kingdom upon this earth. After the rebellion of Satan at Armageddon has been squelched and the Devil is cast into the bottomless pit, Jesus will establish the Kingdom of Righteousness upon this earth. Its capital will be Jerusalem. Israel will be safely regathered in Canaan, the nations will all be subject to the King of Kings. Peace and prosperity will prevail. Every war plant will be dismantled, all military training ended, and the whole world, including even the animal creation, be at peace. There will be no poverty, no discrimination, no class hatred or strife, and no want. Sickness will be unknown, the Gospel will be preached to all men, and all the resources of this earth converted into channels of blessing and usefulness to mankind. It will be the final answer to the prayer which Jesus taught His disciples but which today still awaits fulfillment, "Thy kingdom come. Thy will be done on earth as it is in heaven." Then the prophecy uttered by the angels at Jesus' first coming but not fulfilled up until now, will find its consummation, "Peace on earth, good will among men." This is the glorious age of which we sing when

> Jesus shall reign where'er the sun
> Doth his successive journeys run;
> His Kingdom stretch from shore to shore,
> Till moons shall wax and wane no more.

This then is Event Number 5, The Millennial Kingdom, and will last for one thousand blessed years. And then, to finally prove the utter depravity of human nature, there will be a brief time of rebellion, when Satan shall be loosed for a moment, to be immediately destroyed by fire from Heaven and be cast forever into the lake of fire. It is described:

And when the thousand years are expired, Satan shall be loosed out of his prison,

And shall go out to deceive the nations which are in the four quarters of the earth . . . to gather them together to battle. . . .

. . . and fire came down from God out of heaven, and devoured them (Revelation 20:7-9).

This is EVENT NUMBER SIX, and is followed by EVENT NUMBER SEVEN. It is the number of perfection and of completion.

It will wind up God's program for this world. It is the final judgment of the wicked. At the first coming of Jesus at the beginning of the Tribulation, only saved believers are raised. The rest of the dead — the wicked — are not raised until after the thousand years are finished. But now they appear before the judgment of the Great White Throne. John in Revelation 20, verse 5, tells us: "But the rest of the dead lived not again until the thousand years were finished. . . ."

And in verse 11,

And I saw a great white throne, and him that sat on it. . . .

And I saw the dead [the wicked dead, who were raised at the close of the thousand years] . . . and the dead were judged out of those things which were written in the books, according to their works.

And whosoever was not found written in the book of life was cast into the lake of fire (Revelation 20:11, 12, 15).

And now one other event remains, only one — EVENT NUMBER EIGHT. We have traced the first seven steps so far:

1. The Translation of the Church
2. The Tribulation
3. The Battle of Armageddon
4. The Second Coming of Christ
5. The Millennial Kingdom
6. Satan's Last Rebellion
7. The Last Judgment

With Number 7 God's judgments are completed, and now all things are to be made new. Number 8, therefore, is the number of new things. So this last event, Number 8, sees all things made new. After the wicked have been judged and cast into Hell with Satan, God will usher in *eternity,* an eternity of never-ending perfection. John says:

And I saw a new heaven and a new earth: for the first heaven and the first earth were passed away. . . .

And he that sat upon the throne said, Behold, I make all things new . . . (Revelation 21:1, 5).

Peter tells us God will purify this earth with fire, and out of it will come a new cleansed earth with every vestige and memory of sin forever removed. We shall enjoy the fellowship of the saints of God forever and ever. We will dwell in perfect communion with God in Christ, for God Himself shall be with them and be their God. It is described as follows: "And God shall wipe away all tears . . . and there shall be no more death, neither sorrow, nor crying, neither shall there be any more pain . . ." (Revelation 21:4).

This is the glorious prospect before the child of God, and seeing this, we can truly say with Paul: "For I reckon that the sufferings of this present time are not worthy to be compared with the glory which shall be revealed in us" (Romans 8:18).

Soon this glory will appear. Jesus Himself said: "And when these things begin to come to pass, then look up, and lift up your heads; for your redemption draweth nigh" (Luke 21:28).

For the believer all is bright. There need be no apprehension, no fear, no doubt whatsoever, because we have the sure promise of the Word of God and His program is running on schedule and on time. Our only responsibility is to be faithful in the uncertain time which is left in proclaiming and sending forth the message of the Gospel of the Grace of God. And then with John, the writer of Revelation, we can join in the last prayer of the Bible, "Even so, come, Lord Jesus" (Revelation 22:20).

Chapter Two

THE FIRST MESSAGE FROM HEAVEN

When they therefore were come together they asked
of him, saying, Lord, wilt thou at this time restore
again the kingdom to Israel? (Acts 1:6).

This was the last question which the disciples of our Lord asked our Saviour while here upon the earth. It was a question born of a mixture of eager expectation and shattered hopes. "Wilt thou at *this time* restore again the kingdom to Israel?" This was the question uppermost in the minds of the disciples at this particular moment. They had confidently expected, as all the devout Jews of that day had, that when the Messiah came, He would set up the long-awaited, Messianic Kingdom upon this earth. All the prophets had foretold that when the Messiah should come, Israel would be delivered from the Gentile yoke, the Kingdom of David would be established, and earth's millennial peace would be ushered in.

They as yet, of course, knew nothing about the intervening church age between the First and Second Comings of this Messiah. They did not look for a rejected, crucified Saviour, but a victorious, conquering One to deliver Israel from the cruel yoke of bondage and oppression, and restore the glory of the Kingdom of Israel, foreshadowed by the reigns of David and of King Solomon.

It was this faith in Jesus as the Messiah, that had prompted them to leave all and to follow Him. Even John the Baptist believed that Jesus would deliver Israel but when he was cast into prison, and Jesus did not set up the Kingdom as he expected, he began to doubt, and sent his disciples with the question, "Art thou he (the Messiah) that should come, or look we for another?" But John and the disciples were in for a rude shock, for instead of delivering Israel from bondage, instead of sitting upon the Throne of David, as all the prophets had foretold, Jesus goes instead to the cross and dies as a criminal upon the cruel tree. All their hopes of the Kingdom

21

were shattered and dashed in pieces in a moment and they had all fled in fear. But we can hardly blame the disciples for leaving Him and fleeing in terror at that critical moment, for they as yet knew not the meaning of Calvary. For three days they had lived in complete frustration. But then came a surprise, and their hopes were revived, for He arose. They again took courage. Surely *now* He would set up the Kingdom, after His resurrection. But no — again they must be disappointed, and the next forty days Jesus spent with them talking about the Kingdom, but doing absolutely nothing about it. Then at the end of those forty days Jesus leads them to the Mount of Olives, the very place where the prophets had foretold that the Messiah would come to set up the *kingdom* upon the earth (Zechariah 14:4). The same Mountain where Peter, James and John had seen a vision of the glory of His Kingdom in the transfiguration (Matthew 17). Surely, they thought, now at last He is about to set up the Throne of David, and so they ask the question: "Lord, wilt thou *at this time* restore again the kingdom to Israel?" (Acts 1:6).

Three words arrest our attention in this verse — *at this time.* They knew if God's Word were true that *some day* Messiah would set up the Kingdom. Of this fact they were certain. Could *this* be the time of which the prophets had spoken? And so they ask, "Lord, wilt thou *at this time* restore again the kingdom to Israel?" But instead of a definite answer to this question which Jesus might have given, He merely assures them that it is not the time and it is not for them to know exactly *when* this should occur, and so He says: "It is not for you to know the times or the seasons, which the Father hath put in his own power" (Acts 1:7).

Now this is a tremendously important verse. If, as the majority of professing Christendom teaches today, Jesus is not going to reign on this earth, and the Church is the Kingdom, and all the prophecies concerning the Messianic earthly Kingdom of our Lord must be spiritualized and applied to the Church, and God is all through with national Israel, then right here certainly was the place for Jesus to set His disciples, and all of us, straight on this subject. If God is all through with Israel, and the Church is now spiritual Israel, then this was the opportunity for Jesus to state that fact clearly so that there would be no question, no more misunderstanding or confusion about it. He could have said, for instance, "Forget about the Kingdom. The Church is the Kingdom. God is all through with the Nation of Israel, and they will never return literally to the land." This would have cleared up the matter and prevented all the confusion about this question today. But instead Jesus says, "The *time* is not for you to know." Just wait until Pentecost and the Holy Spirit will give you instructions and further information on what you are to do in the interim, before I set up the Kingdom, for all the promises will still come true.

And then came the shock of their lives. Jesus, after assuring them in this way that the Kingdom would be set up ultimately, suddenly leaves them, and we read: "And when he had spoken these things, while they beheld, he was taken up; and a cloud received him out of their sight" (Acts 1:9).

Their Lord is gone. The King has departed. And their hopes are shattered once more, and come tumbling down like a house of paper about their heads. Just after He had them all keyed up to a high pitch, with the assurance that the Kingdom was not forgotten and it will come, He suddenly disappears from their midst, and they are struck dumb. No one utters a single word; their grief is too great for expression. All they could do was stand and gaze in despair and wonder, and we read that they, ". . . looked stedfastly toward heaven as he went up . . ." (Acts 1:10).

Not a word is spoken. Their King is gone. Is this the end? Is He gone to stay? One can imagine the consternation. And then follows the climax of the entire scene, for while they looked stedfastly toward Heaven as He went up.

BEHOLD

. . . behold, two men stood by them in white apparel (Acts 1:10).

The Lord was gone. Jesus had departed, but He had immediately dispatched two men with a message from Heaven for them. Jesus knew what loneliness of despair must have gripped the hearts of those disciples as He disappears into the blue, and so without delay, He sends back His very first message from Heaven. And what a message it was — a message that dispelled their fears, assured their doubting hearts, rekindled all their hopes, and caused them to return to Jerusalem, the city of the King, to await the next heavenly messenger, the Holy Spirit at Pentecost, and to go forth to turn the world upside down.

JESUS' FIRST MESSAGE

Now notice the content of this first message, the *very first* message our ascended Lord ever sent back from Heaven, to His disciples. Here it is:

. . . two men stood by them in white apparel;
  Which also said, Ye men of Galilee, why stand ye gazing up into heaven? this same Jesus, which is taken up
from you into heaven, shall so come in like manner as ye
have seen him go into heaven (Acts 1:10, 11).

This then was our Lord's first message from Heaven after His
ascension. I AM COMING BACK AGAIN! I WILL RETURN, and when
I do, then the Kingdom promises still will all be fulfilled without
a single exception.

THE CERTAINTY

Yes, indeed, Jesus Christ is coming again. He is coming literally, visibly, bodily, in like manner as He has gone away. The
fact is absolutely certain, while the *time* has not yet been revealed. If Jesus had told His disciples and us the date, the exact
moment of His return, He would have robbed the truth of Christ's
Second Coming of all of its power, its incentive, and its blessing.
It is the imminency of His return which gives to the Second Coming of Christ the power and comfort which it contains. It is the
certainty of the fact and *un*certainty of the time which is the
great incentive to watch. Jesus will return some day, and He
may return today. The early disciples expected our Lord's return
momentarily, and we today have a perfect right to look for Him
to come at any moment. To delay our Lord's return by asserting
that this or that event must first take place is severely condemned
by Jesus Himself. To say that we must have a great world
revival before the Lord can come back again is delaying His
coming. It implies that Christ cannot come today, and it robs
the coming of Christ of its imminency. To teach that we must
see another world war or that Russia must first invade Palestine
before the Lord's return, is to be guilty of delaying the coming
of the Lord, for we then imply that Jesus cannot come until *after*
that event has taken place, and therefore He could *not* come today. This is delaying the Lord's coming. To teach that the
Church must pass through all or part of the Tribulation is delaying the Lord's coming, for if the Church must pass through
only one day of the Tribulation, then we cannot look for Him
until after that day, and therefore Jesus cannot come today. Oh,
let us beware of delaying the Lord's return, of putting it off.
Our Lord said, "It is not for you to know the times or the seasons,"
and He certainly implied by this that we are to look for Him
all the time and at *any* time.

DIRE WARNINGS

In view of the many strange teachings and deceptions so prevalent today concerning the time of our Lord's return, a warning needs to be sounded. To place anything, any event, before our Lord's return is a terrible sin, which will be severely judged. To state that anything must still happen before our Lord comes back is to destroy the imminency and the power of the Second Coming and to take away the incentive for holiness, for service and for patience which the imminent, any-moment expectation of our Lord promotes. To all who would therefore have us believe that something, no matter what it may be, must still occur before we can look for our Lord's return, I would like to quote the words of our Lord:

> But and if that servant say in his heart, My lord delayeth his coming; and shall begin to beat the menservants and maidens, and to eat and drink, and to be drunken;
>
> The lord of that servant will come in a day when he looketh not for him, and at an hour when he is not aware, and will cut him in sunder, and will appoint him his portion with the unbelievers (Luke 12:45, 46).

What a solemn warning to those who deny the possibility of His any-moment return. Jesus *may* come today. If we really believe that He might come before tomorrow morning, it would stir us to the very depths of our souls, I am sure. There would be some things that we have left undone, that we would want to do before we meet Him. There are some things that we have done, that we would want to make right before the Lord's return to call us before the Judgment Seat of Christ. We would live such lives that not a finger could be laid upon us because we would be found working for Him. Surely if we really believed with all our hearts that the Lord Jesus Christ might come back again before another day passes, it would stir us to action. It would cause holiness of walk and conduct and conversation. We would make this last day really count for our Lord and Saviour Jesus Christ. And so we ask the question in closing, "How real is this blessed hope of our Lord's return?" The Apostle John tells us very definitely concerning this:

> And every man that hath this hope in him purifieth himself, even as he is pure (I John 3:3).
>
> Watch therefore: for ye know not what hour your Lord doth come (Matthew 24:42).

Chapter Three

GOD'S LAST PROMISE

He which testifieth these things saith, Surely I come quickly. Amen. Even so, come, Lord Jesus (Revelation 22:20).

In this verse, the very next to the last verse in the entire Bible, we find two last things spoken of. First, we have the last promise, and then we have the last prayer in the Bible. The last promise is from our risen, ascended Lord; the last prayer is by His waiting, redeemed people on the earth, and both of these, the last promise and the last prayer, have to do with just one single thing — the coming again of our Lord Jesus Christ, the only answer to the world's problems, the only hope of a groaning creation, the blessed hope of the waiting Bride. The promise is, "Surely I come quickly." And the prayer is, "Even so, come, Lord Jesus."

IMPORTANT DOCTRINE

The unique way, therefore, in which the Bible closes is in itself an indication of the tremendous importance of the doctrine of the Second Coming of the Lord Jesus Christ. It is important to see this. Last words are always precious words, important words, meaningful words. If you, for instance, knew that you had only a few more minutes to spend with your loved ones here on earth, you certainly would not spend those minutes in idle conversation or inconsequential chatter. You would weigh every word, you would speak of the thing that is nearest and dearest and heaviest upon your heart. The same certainty must have been true of our Lord Jesus Christ, for when He spoke these last words, He knew that this was the end of His revelation to us in the Bible, and in these last few words He speaks of the thing which is closest to His own heart, His Second Coming again, the climax of His redemptive program.

Let those who tell us that the doctrine of the Second Coming of Christ is not an important doctrine, a vital doctrine, a fundamental doctrine, consider this fact, that our Lord in His very last closing words to the waiting Church chose to speak only of His coming again. We have before called your attention to the first message which Jesus ever sent back from Heaven *after* He ascended. It was, "I am coming again" (Acts 1:11). This was the first promise of our ascended Lord, and just as His *first* word *after* He went to Heaven was, "I am coming back again," so the very *last* word which He sent down from Heaven before the canon of Scriptures was closed is again, "I am coming back again." And between these two verses, the first and the last words of our ascended Lord from Heaven, there are more than three hundred references to this blessed, glorious hope in the New Testament, from the first chapter of Acts to the end of the book of the Revelation.

MUST BE PREACHED

Considering, therefore, the importance attached by the Holy Spirit and the Lord Jesus Christ to this great truth as indicated by the space and the prominence given to it in the writings of Paul, John, James, Peter and Jude, we wonder why it is preached so seldom in many, many quarters. A preacher friend said to me, "I never preach on the Second Coming, for I do not consider it a fundamental or important doctrine." What a serious indictment, what a charge to hurl against the blessed person of the Holy Spirit, who devotes so much space to it in the Bible, and gives it such an important place. What an accusation against the apostles who constantly preached it, and the writers of the Bible who ceaselessly proclaimed it.

It is a fact that far more is said concerning the glorious Second Coming of Christ in the Old Testament than about His first coming in humiliation, for without His Second Coming, the first is sterile, abortive, barren and incomplete. Read the Old Testament and you will find many more references to the Lord's glorious Second Coming and the setting up of His Kingdom than to His first coming in humiliation at Calvary. No wonder that the people of Israel lost sight of the first coming amidst the mass of revelation concerning His Second Coming. As a result, almost everyone, including the disciples and even John the Baptist, expected that when the Messiah would come, He would set up His Kingdom in glory. And so when He came nineteen hundred years ago, and the revelation of the cross was given, it was to them a great, a tremendous shock and a terrible disappointment. And just as Israel was at that time so occupied with the glory of Messiah's Kingdom that they failed to consider and lost sight of the cross which must precede it, so today I fear that there are many so occupied with the cross and His first coming that they have lost sight of the value and the necessity and the meaning of His Second Coming to set up the Kingdom. We would not in any way minimize the importance of the cross, but without the Second Coming the entire plan remains incomplete. And so the Jews of Jesus' day knew only Kingdom truth and nothing about the Church. Today the very opposite is true, and the mass of Christendom sees only the Church, and knows nothing about the Kingdom truth of our Lord's return.

CONSIDER ITS PROMINENCE

Do you realize that the very first promise that God ever gave to man after he fell was the promise of the Second Coming of the Messiah? In Genesis 3:15 God in pronouncing judgment upon the serpent immediately after Adam's fall, says: "And I will put enmity between thee and the woman, and between thy seed and her seed; it shall bruise thy head, and thou shalt bruise his heel" (Genesis 3:15).

Now everyone knows and everyone agrees that this promise refers to the coming of the Redeemer, the seed of the woman, but have you ever seen the two comings of the Redeemer in this verse? They are both very clearly there. Here is the first coming: "Thou [the seed of the serpent] shalt bruise his [the seed of the woman] heel."

Now this, everyone agrees, is already history. It was literally fulfilled nineteen hundred years ago when Jesus hung upon the cross with His feet nailed to a literal tree, and His heel literally bruised by the emissaries of the serpent, Satan.

But this verse (Genesis 3:15) contains more than the bruising of the Saviour's heel. It also speaks of the crushing of the serpent's head, which of course, means his final end, for when the head is crushed that means the end of his existence. It refers, therefore, to the ultimate, complete, and final victory of our Lord Jesus Christ over Satan. At our Lord's first coming His heel was bruised, but it will only be at His Second Coming that Satan's head will be finally crushed and bruised and complete victory for the Saviour be assured.

To say that this prophecy of the crushing of Satan's head was fulfilled at Calvary is to ignore the plain teaching of the Word of God. Listen to Paul who gives us the answer: "And the God of peace shall bruise Satan under your feet shortly . . ." (Romans 16:20).

Now this was written by the Apostle Paul some thirty years after Calvary, and Paul tells us the bruising of Satan is still in the future. Certainly if Jesus is not coming back again, then Calvary was a victory for Satan instead of for the Lord Jesus Christ. How significant, therefore, that the very first promise in the Old Testament includes both the first coming when the Saviour's heel would be bruised, but also the Second Coming when He will crush the serpent's head.

CLOSE OF THE OLD TESTAMENT

But even more astonishing is the fact that the very last promise in the Old Testament was also the promise — not of our Lord's first coming, but of His second. We, of course, do not underestimate the importance of our Lord's first advent, to suffer, to die, and to rise again. We would not make His Second Coming more important than His first, for they are inseparable and of equal importance. The first coming is incomplete without His second, and the second is impossible without the first. We merely want to emphasize how important our Lord's return is, how absolutely essential in the final consummation of the redemption which He began at Calvary and will complete when He comes again. And so consider the last promise in the Old Testament. You will find it in Malachi, chapter 4, verse 1, where we read:

> For, behold, the day cometh, that shall burn as an oven; and all the proud, yea, and all that do wickedly, shall be stubble: and the day that cometh shall burn them up, saith the LORD of hosts, that it shall leave them neither root nor branch (Malachi 4:1).

Now the teaching of this passage is unmistakable. Malachi, of course, is referring to the "day of the Lord," an expression occurring hundreds of times in the Scriptures and without exception refers to that awful day of earth's judgment which will be ushered in at the coming of Christ for His Church. It is called not only the "day of the Lord" but also the "great tribulation," the "day of vengeance of our God," the "time of Jacob's trouble," and many other equally descriptive titles.

And then, notice verse 2 of Malachi 4: "But unto you that fear my name shall the Sun of righteousness arise with healing in his wings . . ." (Malachi 4:2).

This is a clear, definite reference to the return of our Lord Jesus Christ as the "Sun of righteousness" to dispel the darkness and the gloom of this present age. To the Nation of Israel, the Messiah Jesus will come as the Sun of Righteousness to dispel the darkness of the time of Jacob's trouble, during the Tribulation. Malachi describes this day:

> Behold, I will send my messenger, and he shall prepare the way before me: and the Lord, whom ye seek, shall suddenly come to his temple, even the messenger of the covenant, whom ye delight in: behold, he shall come, saith the LORD of hosts.
>
> But who may abide the day of his coming? and who shall stand when he appeareth? for he is like a refiner's fire, and like fullers' soap:
>
> And he shall sit as a refiner and purifier of silver: and he shall purify the sons of Levi, and purge them as gold and silver, that they may offer unto the LORD an offering in righteousness.
>
> Then shall the offering of Judah and Jerusalem be pleasant unto the LORD, as in the days of old, and as in former years (Malachi 3:1-4).

When the earth's darkest moment arrives, it will only be by the coming of the Lord that her problems will be solved and peace and righteousness will be ushered in.

THE MORNING STAR

But just exactly as Christ will come *after* the Tribulation to the Nation of Israel as the Sun of Righteousness to deliver them, just so He will *first* come as the Morning Star to catch away His Church. We read:

> And he that overcometh, and keepeth my works unto the end, to him will I give power over the nations:
>
> And he shall rule them with a rod of iron; as the vessels of a potter shall they be broken to shivers: even as I received of my Father.
>
> *And I will give him the morning star* (Revelation 2:26-28).

This glorious promise of the Morning Star is addressed to the Church, His waiting Bride. But to Israel He is presented as the Sun of Righteousness. Now the figure is most suggestive and instructive. The morning star is one of the brightest stars

in the heavens. It always arises shortly before the dawn and
is followed by the darkest hour of the entire night, the hour
just before the dawn. The morning star heralds the night's
darkest hour, but also proclaims the promise of the soon coming sunrise. And then after this darkest period of the night,
after the morning star arises, the sun shows itself, dispelling the
darkness, awaking all nature, and bringing in a new day.

This is the Bible revelation concerning our Lord's return also.
The next event is the rising of the morning star for the Church
when Jesus comes from

> . . . heaven with a shout, with the voice of the archangel,
> and with the trump of God: and the dead in Christ shall
> rise first:
>   Then we which are alive and remain shall be caught
> up together with them in the clouds, to meet the Lord in
> the air: and so shall we ever be with the Lord (I Thessa-
> lonians 4:16, 17).

And then after this event of the Rapture of the Church will
come the Tribulation, the Day of the Lord, the time of Jacob's
trouble, and earth's bath of blood, the blackest period in human
history, a time of suffering so intense that Jesus said: "Except
those days were shortened there should no flesh be saved."
And then after this period of seven years, when everything
seems to be lost, the Sun of Righteousness, the Lord Jesus
Christ, will suddenly return with His glorified Bride, the Church,
and usher in the glad millennial day of earth's redemption,
Israel's restoration, and universal blessing upon all nations of
the earth, when

> Christ shall have dominion,
> Over land and sea;
> Earth's remotest regions,
> Shall His empires be.

This, beloved, is the program of God. This is the only hope
of the world, for the nations, and for creation. The next event
on the program in the schedule of God, is that glorious event,
called also "that blessed hope," when the Lord Jesus Himself
will return according to the promise of His Book: "He which
testifieth these things saith, Surely I come quickly. Amen . . ."
(Revelation 22:20).

May our hearts respond, "Even so, come, Lord Jesus."

Chapter Four

DENY — DELAY — DEBAUCH

*For the grace of God that bringeth salvation hath
appeared to all men,*
*Teaching us that, denying ungodliness and worldly
lusts, we should live soberly, righteously, and godly,
in this present world;*
*Looking for that blessed hope, and the glorious ap-
pearing of the great God and our Saviour Jesus Christ;*
*Who gave himself for us, that he might redeem
us from all iniquity, and purify unto himself a peculiar
people, zealous of good works.*
*These things speak, and exhort, and rebuke with
all authority. Let no man despise thee* (Titus 2:11-15).

All true Christians believe in the "fact" of Christ's return,
but they are by no means agreed on the details. On this there
is endless disagreement and confusion. Some teach that Christ
will return at the end of the world; others believe that He will
come before the Millennium. Some teach that Christ will return for His Church before the Tribulation, while others teach
that He will return at the end of the Tribulation period. Some
believe and teach that only sanctified believers will be raptured, and that the carnal Christians will pass through the
tribulation fires. Some are pre-millennial, some post-millennial,
some a-millennial, some hold to a pre-tribulation rapture, others
to a post-tribulation rapture, and still others hold to a mid-
tribulation rapture.

CONFUSING

As a result of all of this confusion and misunderstanding,
there are many Christians who make an excuse for neglecting
the study of this great truth, and we oftentimes hear men say,
"This is all so terribly confusing that we have given up the
study of the Second Coming entirely, since there seems to be
no agreement even among Bible scholars on this particular

matter." Various ones have told me personally, "I don't bother about the Second Coming of Christ, because even Bible students cannot come to a place of general agreement, so I have just ignored the subject entirely."

This is just exactly what the Devil wants you to do, and that is the reason why he has caused all this confusion. That is why the enemy rejoices over all of this misunderstanding among believers, for the Devil himself knows the tremendous importance of this truth and will do everything in his power to keep believers in darkness and ignorance concerning "that blessed hope." If there is one truth, one doctrine, one teaching in the Bible which the Devil would keep away from the believer, it is the Bible revelation concerning our Lord's return. The hatred of Satan for this great and vital doctrine in itself only proves how important the Devil knows and considers it to be. And so instead of discouraging us in our studies, the very confusion which Satan has produced should serve to increase our interest and determination to study it more than ever, that we may arrive at the real truth of the Scriptures.

THREE-FOLD ATTACK

Now Satan, the enemy of the truth, in seeking to rob us of the blessing of the hope of Christ's return, usually follows three carefully planned lines of attack. First of all, he seeks to get men to *deny* the "fact" of Christ's return. This is the modern view of the infidel and the unbeliever. He denies the fact that Christ is even coming back again in person. He either denies it outright, or he denies it by spiritualizing the promises of our Lord's return, and thus destroying it by teaching that Christ has already returned, at Pentecost, or at the destruction of Jerusalem, while still others teach that conversion is the second coming, or that death is our Lord's return. To all such who hold these different claims, we merely would like to quote the words of the Bible itself: ". . . THIS SAME JESUS, which is taken up from you into heaven, shall so come in like manner as ye have seen him go into heaven" (Acts 1:11).

SECOND PERVERSION

But this first attack of Satan fails to deceive the true believer. The true believer knows the fact of Christ's personal return cannot be denied without destroying the entire Scriptures, and so Satan pursues quite another course for those who accept the *fact* of the Lord's coming again. If he cannot make us deny the literal return of Christ, then he seeks to make us *delay* this blessed event. Like the servant in Luke 12 who said in his heart, "My lord delayeth his coming," so also there are many today who believe that Jesus *is* coming back, but they put it off and project it into the far-distant and irrelevant future. It is to them a doctrine, not a life; an article of faith without the life of faith; a statement of creed instead of a living incentive as a blessed hope, a continual expectation, and a transforming power. Since Christ is not expected in the near future, and possibly not even in our lifetime, but His coming again lies somewhere in the dim, faraway days ahead, it becomes just a lifeless doctrine, a dead creed, a sterile dogma. Unless the hope of Christ's return can be narrowed down, and brought down to the possibility of today, it ceases to be the purifying hope.

We are constantly admonished in the Scriptures over and over again, to "look for His appearing." How can we, beloved, look for it if it will not occur until way off in the future? Looking for an event or person implies that we are expecting it and waiting for it. Paul tells us that those who would live soberly, righteously, and godly in this present world are "looking for that blessed hope, and the glorious appearing of the great God and our Saviour Jesus Christ" (Titus 2:13).

Are you looking for Him, or do you put it off to some other day? The very fact that our Lord would not reveal the time of His return was for the very purpose of keeping us constantly on the alert and on the look-out for Him. Suppose the Lord had said, "I'll come back again in 1961." It would have meant little to the early Christians. Or suppose that He had said, "I'll be back in 1963." Even then it would mean little to us today, for we would still have more than a whole year to get ready, and would undoubtedly put it off until the last moment. But now, since we are to look for Him every day, and that hour is unknown, because we know not the day nor the hour, it becomes an incentive to live our lives every day as though it might be our very last before the Lord returns.

THIRD DECEPTION

This brings us to a third deception of the enemy. We have called it *debauching* the truth of the Second Coming. If the Devil cannot get us to *deny* His coming again, and then cannot tempt us to *delay* His return, then he seeks to get folks to corrupt and to *debauch* this truth by all sorts of foolish and fanatical interpretations, unscriptural claims concerning the time of His coming. Setting of days, and dates, pin-pointing the time when Jesus must come, is *debauching* the truth. People who are otherwise orthodox, zealous, will be deceived by Satan in setting the time, and then when it fails to happen, the whole truth of Christ's return is brought into disrepute and reproach. Let us beware of *denying*, *delaying* and *debauching* the truth of the Second Coming of Christ.

The Worst Error of All

The most severe condemnation of our Lord, however, falls not upon those who because of their ignorance of God's Word fall into the foolishness of setting dates, but rather upon those who say in their hearts, "My lord *delayeth* his coming." In Luke 12 our Lord tells us the severe judgment which awaits all those who dare to put off the coming of the Lord. Of course, we cannot actually "delay" the return of the Lord, for "he that shall come will come, and will not tarry" (Hebrews 10:37). This, of course, is not the meaning of the unfaithful servant's words, "My lord delayeth his coming." It is quite impossible for us to change God's plan, and when the time for Christ to come is here, He of course will come. But the meaning is rather that this servant denied the imminency of his lord's return, and that he could not come at that particular moment. He said *in his heart*, "My lord delayeth his coming." We emphasize here once more the fact that this servant *did not deny* the fact of his lord's return. He believed it. He believed that the lord would come back again, but he did not believe that it would or could be today. That was his error — living as though the lord would come at some future time, but his coming was neither imminent nor near, and had no impact or influence upon him at that particular moment. He imagined there were still many things to happen before the lord would be coming back.

Modern Application

Now this mistake of the servant in Luke 12 is a common mistake. Countless people who believe that Christ will return and are as orthodox as they can be, nevertheless live as though they were quite sure that it is still a long way off. They tell us that we are to look for this or that event to happen before the return of the Lord. This teaching, that something must still occur before the Lord can return, is really saying in your heart, "My Lord delayeth His coming." We hear much about revival today, and thank God for every sign of a reviving among the people of God; thank God for the souls which are being saved; we are for it, and if the Lord does not come soon, may it increase, but to say that we *must* have a great revival before the Lord comes is saying in your heart, "My Lord delayeth His coming." To say that the world must be evangelized before the Lord can come back again is to delay His coming until after that has been accomplished. It is delaying the Lord's coming. We are nowhere told to look for revival, but to look for the Lord's return instead. Revival is not the hope of this world. Revival is not the final answer to the world's problems. Its only hope is the coming of the Lord in this dispensation. There is not one verse in the entire Scripture which even hints that we will have a great worldwide revival before the Lord returns for His Church, and I fear that today we have become so interested in revival that we are losing sight of our only ultimate hope, the return of the Lord Jesus Christ.

Our Only Hope

The Bible therefore holds out only one solution for this troubled world, one permanent answer to the problems of the entire creation. And that answer is the return of the King whose right it is to reign. We repeat, therefore, there is no greater incentive for revival, for holiness, for evangelism, than the conviction of our Lord's imminent coming again. If we, therefore, really believed that Jesus might come before tomorrow, if we really believed it, it would result in such activity as we have never seen before in all our lives. If we were convinced that this was our last day upon the earth before we were to meet Him, how it would stir us to our very heart's depths, to win our loved ones to Christ before it is too late. How it would cause us to make some things right before He comes, to do some things we intended to do but didn't do because we thought we would have some more time later on.

Someone has said that we ought so to live as though Christ were crucified yesterday, that He arose this morning, and that He is coming back again tonight. This is the power of that blessed hope, this is the result of the expectation of our Lord. And listen, my friend, one of these days it is really, actually going to happen. No matter how long it may be, or how soon, He *is* coming again. *Some day*, it may be today, the Lord will come, according to His promise. To deny it is to say in your heart, "My Lord delayeth His coming."

O God, deliver us from a lifeless creed, a dead dogma, a dry doctrine, a mere statement of faith, and a powerless profession! Help us so to conduct our lives, so to work to win others, that if Jesus should come, there would be no regrets on our part. May that be our constant prayer as we live in the atmosphere of "looking for that blessed hope, and the glorious appearing of the great God and our Saviour Jesus Christ."

Just one thought in conclusion. We constantly hear the objection from well-meaning and sincere Christians that they cannot sincerely pray for the coming of the Lord and wish that He might return immediately because there are so many unsaved loved ones who have not yet received the Lord Jesus Christ. We have but to answer them that the longer the Lord remains away, the more of these there will be, and if we really believe that the Lord might come very soon, we probably would do something definite about winning these who are still without Christ before it is forever too late. Yes, there is no greater incentive to holiness, to soul-winning, to living our lives for Christ, than the hope of the imminent return of our Lord Jesus Christ.

> Jesus may come today,
>   Glad day! Glad day!
> And I would see my Friend;
>   Dangers and troubles would end
> If Jesus should come today.
>
> Glad day! Glad day!
>   Is it the crowning day?
> I'll live for today, nor anxious be,
>   Jesus, my Lord, I soon shall see;
> Glad day! Glad day!
>   Is it the crowning day?

Chapter Five

MEAT IN DUE SEASON

And the Lord said, Who then is that faithful and wise steward, whom his lord shall make ruler over his household, to give them their portion of meat in due season?

Blessed is that servant, whom his lord when he cometh shall find so doing.

Of a truth I say unto you, that he will make him ruler over all that he hath (Luke 12:42-44).

This is one of many, many parables of our Lord concerning His Second Coming. Jesus implies in this narrative that the lord of the house had left for a time, and had committed the feeding of his household to his servants. When he returns he will reward these servants on the basis of their faithfulness in providing meat for the children of the lord at the proper time and in due season. Faithfulness in this matter will be rewarded, according to Jesus' own words: "Blessed is that servant, whom his lord when he cometh shall find so doing" (Luke 12:43).

THE UNFAITHFUL SERVANT

Then follows our Lord's teaching concerning the unfaithful servant who during our Lord's absence withholds from the king's children their food in due season. The penalty is so severe that we want to quote the passage just as we find it:

But and if that servant say in his heart, My lord delayeth his coming; and shall begin to beat the menservants and maidens, and to eat and drink, and to be drunken;

The lord of that servant will come in a day when he looketh not for him, and at an hour when he is not aware, and will cut him in sunder, and will appoint him his portion with the unbelievers (Luke 12:45, 46).

These are solemn words that need to be considered very carefully. A servant of the Lord, cut asunder (cut off) and

given the portion of the "unfaithful ones"! The word translated "unbelievers" may also be rendered "unfaithful ones."
In studying these two verses concerning the unfaithful servant,
we notice a number of things:

1. The man was a servant of the Lord.
2. He neglected his duty.
3. He abused his fellow servants and lived in riotousness.
4. He was severely punished for his sin.
5. The cause of it all was his attitude toward the return
   of the Lord Jesus Christ.

First of all then, will you notice that this man was a servant
of the Lord. Jesus after speaking of the faithful servant who
was to be rewarded says: "But and if *that* servant say in his
heart, My lord delayeth his coming . . ." (Luke 12:45).

Now the important word is *that:* "But and if *that* servant
say in his heart." Jesus, of course, refers to the same servant
who had been faithful in the first place. It is not another
servant, but the same one, who can either be faithful, or unfaithful in this charge which the Lord committed to him.
In verses 42 to 44, Jesus tells us what will happen to the *faithful* servant. In verses 45 and 46 He tells us what will happen
if he, this same servant, is *unfaithful*. What happens to this
man, therefore, can happen to the servant of the Lord.

Secondly, will you notice that he neglected his duty? His
job was to give to the Lord's household their portion of *meat*
in due season. It is the servant of the Lord's duty to regularly,
constantly, give the children of God the milk and the meat
of the Word of the Lord; not entertainment, not stories, not
political discourses, moralizations, not economical discussions,
but the *meat*. Meat in due season, says our Lord. And the
true minister of God is obligated to feed God's people *meat*,
the solid meat of the Word, and that includes the meat of the
truth of Christ's return. Neglect to do so necessitates the judgment of Almighty God. From the context, therefore, we gather
that this was the servant's greatest failure — neglect to regard and declare the truth of the Lord's return. He made light
of our Lord's coming again, and was guilty of delaying the
Lord's coming.

The third thing was his conduct toward his fellow servants.
He beat them and abused them. Now this is always the re-
sult of neglecting and postponing the coming of the Lord.
There is nothing in all the world which can produce holiness

of life, charity in conduct, fervent evangelism, like the daily expectation of the imminent return of our Lord. If this servant had expected the Lord to return at any moment, he would not have conducted himself as he did. It was only because he said in his heart, "My lord delayeth his coming," that he began to beat the servants and to live in sinful worldliness.

ORTHODOXY AND SPIRITUALITY

Evidently this servant was orthodox but very unspiritual. A man may be as orthodox as the Devil himself, and yet be as dead spiritually as a dodo. A Christian may be straight on the Gospel in every respect, and know the doctrines from beginning to end, and be able to split theological hairs in quarters, and yet be as cold, unspiritual and useless as a dead fish. The test of orthodoxy is merely this: "What do you believe concerning the first coming of Christ?" If a man or a church believes in the virgin birth, the supernatural conception of our Lord, His sinless life, His deity, His atoning death, and His bodily resurrection, such a man or church, of course, is considered thoroughly orthodox. But with all that orthodoxy, they may still be as cold, as critical, as unloving, as indifferent, as worldly as the servant in our parable. A person's theology can be as clear as ice and twice as cold.

SPIRITUALITY

But just as the test of orthodoxy is one's belief concerning Christ's *first* coming, the test of spirituality is this: "What do you believe concerning Christ's *Second* Coming?" Show me a man or a church or an assembly which truly believes in the personal, imminent return of Christ at any moment, and I will show you a man or an assembly that is spiritually on fire, striving for holiness, ablaze with zeal for souls, and fired with the spirit of evangelism. It cannot be otherwise, for if we really believe that Jesus may come at any moment, if we really believe this in our heart of hearts, it must result in a zeal to be doing His will when He comes. History records that practically all the really God-honored and God-used evangelists have been firm believers in the imminent, pre-millennial return of the Lord Jesus Christ. John tells us in his first epistle: "And every man that hath this hope in him [that is, the hope of Christ's return] purifieth himself, even as he is pure" (I John 3:3).

THE SERVANT'S MISTAKE

And that brings us to the very heart of our lesson of this unfaithful servant. All of his abuse of his fellow servants, his eating, his drinking, his intolerance, his looseness of living, was rooted in one serious error and mistake which he had made. This mistake was his attitude toward the *imminent* return of the Lord Jesus Christ. Jesus says of this servant that he said in his heart "my lord *delayeth* his coming."

This was the fatal mistake which this servant of the Lord made. He did not deny the Second Coming of the Lord Jesus Christ. He did not spiritualize the promises of the return of his Lord. He simply believed it as a fact, as a cold fact, but projected it into the far distant, irrelevant future. He did not deny the fact of his Lord's coming back again, but he denied the possibility of His coming at any moment; that is, he denied its imminency. By the term "imminent" we mean not that He will return today or tomorrow or next year, but that He *may* return at any moment. We do not teach the *immediate* return of the Lord Jesus, but His *imminent* return, that He may return at any moment, and He may return today. We believe that the Lord will return some day. We must distinguish, therefore, between "immediate" and "imminent." Sometimes we have been accused of teaching the "immediate" return of the Lord. Of course, we teach nothing of the kind, but we do believe in His "imminent" coming; that is, that He may come at any moment, and He may even come today.

Now the fault of this unfaithful servant was his denial of the possibility of the Lord's return until sometime in the future, and so he says, "my lord delayeth his coming." We repeat, he did not deny His coming. He seems to say, He is coming back some day, but He is not coming back for a long, long while, and so it had no effect upon his conduct *now;* it made no impact on him at the very moment, because he did not expect his lord until way off in the far-distant future. This was this servant's sin, delaying His coming, or putting it the other way — "denying the imminent return of the Lord," and this resulted in his worldliness and his conduct toward his fellow servants.

THE LORD RETURNS

But what a terrible mistake he made, for we read: "The lord of that servant will come in a day when he looketh not for him, and at an hour when he is not aware . . ." (Luke 12:46).

Rob the truth of Jesus' return of its imminency, and we reduce it to a cold, orthodox, sterile doctrine, an event so far removed from our practical life today, that it does not affect us whatsoever. And that is just what the Devil would like to have us do. He doesn't care if we believe in the return of the Lord. He is not concerned about our orthodoxy on the *fact* of Christ's return, just so long as it remains only a doctrine, an article in our creed, an event which is not of any concern particularly today.

Only as we live in the constant hope and the continued expectation of His return, can it really affect our lives and fire us with zeal for holiness and for evangelism. How real, therefore, my Christian friend, is this "blessed hope" in your life? Do you really believe in the imminent return of our Lord? Do you believe that He could come, He might come, today? Then remember, one of these days He *will* come. Are you sure it cannot be today? Here then is the test. If we really believed that Jesus might come before tomorrow morning, if we really believed this fact, what do you suppose we would do? How would we live? Certainly we would get rid of some things that we know we wouldn't want to be caught with when He returns. Certainly we would make some things right that are still all wrong, things we wouldn't want to be found with when the Lord comes to judge His servants. Certainly we would try to still do some thing that we have neglected to do in the past and have put off until tomorrow. The very fact that Christians continue in their selfishness and pride and unforgiveness, covetousness, worldliness, and indifference, reveals the fact that they do *not* believe the Lord might come before another day passes. They are saying in their hearts like the unfaithful servant, "My lord delayeth his coming." To put off anything that you ought to do today, before He comes, is delaying His coming in your own heart. Of course, we cannot actually delay His coming, for He will come anyway, but in your heart you only think, you deceive yourselves that He will not come yet for a long time, and so men continue in the neglect, but "The lord of that servant will come in a day when he looketh not for him, and at an hour when he is not aware . . ." (Luke 12:46).

How real, my friend, is the hope of the Lord's return to you right this very moment? Is it real enough to make you do something about it, or are you, while you profess to believe in His soon return, denying it by your life and your actions?

Oh, Lord, make this thing real in our lives, so real that it will cause us to bestir ourselves and cleanse our lives from every known and doubtful sin. Make the possibility of Thy return at any moment such a reality in our lives that we shall be gripped by it and shall stop our bickering and criticizing and fault-finding and division, and fighting over unimportant things, make it so real that we shall spend every future moment between now and that imminent event of Thy coming in living for Thee, in cleansing our lives, in winning souls, and helping others, in serving Thee, and heeding the admonition: "Watch ye therefore, and pray always, that ye may be accounted worthy to escape all these things that shall come to pass, and to stand before the Son of man" (Luke 21:36).

Help us to prove Thy Word, which says: ". . . every man that hath this hope in him purifieth himself, even as he is pure" (I John 3:3).

Chapter Six

THE MYSTERY OF THE KINGDOM

It is impossible to understand properly God's program for this age, God's dealings with Israel, the Church and the nations, unless we understand the difference between the Kingdom of Heaven and the Mystery of the Kingdom of Heaven. The Kingdom of Heaven is the literal rule of Heaven's King, the Lord Jesus, on earth. All the Old Testament prophets foretold this coming golden age, and every devout Jew expected this to happen when Messiah came, but when Messiah did come, He did *not* set up His Kingdom but was instead rejected, went to the cross and left without fulfilling the literal promises of His reign. Instead of Israel's Davidic Kingdom being restored, the nation was rejected, their city burned, and the people scattered throughout the world.

This failure of the Messiah to set up the Kingdom was the thing which confused the disciples, and even John the Baptist. The reason for their confusion was due to the fact that they did not understand the *mystery* aspect of the Kingdom of Heaven. Simply stated, the "mystery" they did not understand was this, the King when He came the first time would be rejected, and would go back to Heaven without delivering Israel, and bringing in the Kingdom on earth. Instead of the Kingdom, He would, after His rejection, call out a company from all nations and build a Church, after which He would return and fulfill every promise concerning this golden age. This Church Age between the first and second coming of the King was the mystery which was hidden from their eyes. They knew about the promised Kingdom of Heaven at the coming of Messiah, but did not see the interval between the two comings. The disciples expected Jesus to declare Himself as King and for this very reason the first coming of Jesus as Messiah of Israel was a frustrating disappointment to the Nation of Israel and to His followers. They had earnestly expected the Christ to set up His Kingdom so clearly prophesied in the Scriptures.

44

However, they failed to see that at His first coming He would be rejected, die on the cross, rise and go back to Heaven, and then later to return the second time in glory to fulfill all the Kingdom promises. We repeat, the setting up of the Kingdom was no mystery. The prophecies were replete with glowing descriptions of that coming golden age. This was clear enough, but they failed to see that between His first and second coming lay an age of more than nineteen hundred years during which God would deal, not with the kingdom nation but with another group, the Body of Christ, the Church. Although the prophets clearly foretold the rejection of Christ as well as the glorious reign of the Messiah, the Old Testament prophets and saints failed to see the interval between the two events. This was hidden for a definite reason. The truth of this dispensation of grace, while the Church is being formed, was unknown until after Pentecost. For this reason Jesus was rejected when He came the first time.

PROPHETS DID NOT SEE THIS

Even the Old Testament prophets who foretold both the first and second comings of Messiah failed to see the Church Age between the two. Peter tells us plainly in words which cannot be misunderstood, that the prophets of old did not understand their own words concerning this mystery. Speaking of this present age of the Church he says: "Of which salvation the prophets have inquired and searched diligently, who prophesied of the grace that should come unto you" (I Peter 1:10).

Peter tells us that the prophets of old spoke of this Age of Grace in which we live, but they did not understand what they themselves were saying, and therefore, they inquired and searched diligently of the "grace that should come unto you." Now what did they inquire about? What was it they wanted to know and which they could not understand? Peter gives the answer. He tells us they searched, ". . . what, or what manner of *time* the Spirit of Christ which was in them did signify, when it testified beforehand the *sufferings* of Christ, and the *glory* that should follow" (I Peter 1:11).

We must not hurry over this verse. Old Testament prophets saw in the future the coming of Christ but were confused, because they saw Him both *suffering* and coming in *glory*. How could He both suffer and die, and also be glorified and reign? They saw the two things but failed to see that the *suffering* and *glory* were separated and did not occur at the same time. And so they inquired about "the *time*." It was the "*time* between" which was the mystery and about which they searched diligently. It was the intervening Church Age between the two comings which they could not understand. It was the *mystery* of the Kingdom of Heaven. The Kingdom of Heaven was no mystery, but the "mystery" of the Kingdom, that was something else, for that was God's hidden program for this present dispensation which none of the prophets of old understood. So when they inquired and searched diligently God did reveal something to them, without, however, fully explaining the mystery. So Peter tells us that their question concerning the *time* between the suffering and the glory had to do, not with them (the Kingdom Age) but another company. Hear Peter's words:

> Unto whom it was revealed, that not unto themselves, but unto *us* [who are on this side of Calvary, *unto us*] they did minister the things, which are *now* [since Pentecost] reported unto you by them that have preached the gospel unto you with the Holy Ghost sent down from heaven; which things the angels desire to look into (I Peter 1:12).

The mystery into which they had inquired, had to do with *us*, this side of Calvary, but beyond this they were given no further information. It must remain a mystery even to the angels, a mystery to be revealed in due time.

HIDDEN IN AGES PAST

The Old Testament saints and prophets knew nothing of a Church as the Body of Christ. It was not directly revealed, although today with the light of the New Testament we can see it in type and shadow. The Old Testament dealt almost exclusively with one nation — the Nation of Israel, God's Kingdom nation. Other nations are only mentioned as they had some dealing with this one Kingdom people. All but the first eleven chapters of the thirty-nine books of the Old Testament are occupied with God's chosen people Israel. Genesis records the beginning of the nation through Abraham, Isaac, Jacob and Joseph. Exodus records the early history of the children of Israel in Egypt and their deliverance. Leviticus tells us of the national laws, rituals, offerings, and worship of this one nation. Numbers records the journey of this nation from Egypt

to Canaan. And Deuteronomy deals with the laws and regu-
lations to govern them in the land. Joshua tells of the conquest
of Israel's land. Judges is the record of their early struggles.
Kings and Chronicles are the record of her wars and final ex-
pulsion from the land and dispersion among the nations. The
poetic books deal with the worship of this people, and the
prophetic books are prophecies concerning the future of this
one single nation. Only by distorting the Word of God and
doing violence to its literal meaning can we find the Church in
the Old Testament. We find types and shadows of her in the
history of the nation, but these could only be understood
in the light of the New Testament revelation, but were a dark
mystery until then.

PAUL AND THE MYSTERY

That this Church Age was a mystery is clear from many,
many passages. We read:

> For this cause I Paul, the prisoner of Jesus Christ for you
> Gentiles,
> If ye have heard of the dispensation of the grace of
> God which is given me to you-ward:
> How that by revelation he made known unto me the
> *mystery;* (as I wrote afore in few words,
> Whereby, when ye read, ye may understand my knowl-
> edge in the mystery of Christ) (Ephesians 3:1-4).

Here Paul speaks of the mystery of the "grace of God."
He calls it the dispensation of the "grace of God." This knowledge was given to Paul by special revelation because it was
never revealed before, and so he continues: "Which in other
ages [or dispensations] was not made known unto the sons of
men, as it is now revealed unto his holy apostles and prophets
[of the New Testament] by the Spirit" (Ephesians 3:5).

This mystery had been hidden until the coming of the Spirit
on Pentecost, but was now revealed and manifested to the New
Testament apostles and prophets. And what was the revelation
of this mystery? "That the Gentiles should be fellowheirs, and
of the same body, and partakers of his promise in Christ by
the gospel" (Ephesians 3:6).

Now the secret is out. The Lord in this dispensation (hidden
before) will not limit His dealings to one nation — the Nation
of Israel — but the Gentiles will now also become partakers
of God's special dealings by the Gospel. Up until the day of

Pentecost God was dealing in salvation with the Nation of Israel. To become a member of God's people, one must become a Jew, submit to the rite of circumcision. Truly salvation was of the Jews.

MIDDLE WALL BROKEN DOWN

After Pentecost and the coming of the Holy Spirit, God begins to deal with the Gentiles as well, and begins to call out the Church, the Body of Christ, consisting of both Jews and Gentiles. God ceases to deal with national Israel, and instead is calling out from among the Gentiles a people for His name. This part of God's program was unknown before Pentecost, and we can, therefore, understand why the disciples could not reconcile His death and rejection with the prophecies of the setting up of the Kingdom.

WHY KEPT A SECRET?

But now we face a real problem. Why did God keep this mystery a secret? Why was it not revealed so that when He came the first time they would have recognized Him as the suffering Messiah, who later would come as the glorious King? And right here we come to the real mystery. God in His infinitely wise plan of redemption purposed from eternity to have a redeemed company taken from every people, tribe, and nation to be the Bride of Christ. But in order to redeem them, sin must be put away, and the only way sin could be done away was by the death and shedding of the blood of the Redeemer. Before He can redeem, He must die. He must die an atoning, substitutionary death. To be the Redeemer of the worst sinner, He must die the death of the worst criminal. This death was by crucifixion, the one mode of death reserved only for the vilest of criminals. Someone, therefore, must be used to put the Redeemer to death. And God chose the Nation of Israel, out of whom the Redeemer was to come, and through whom the Redeemer was to die. In the eternal counsels of God, He planned the death of His Son at the hands of His chosen nation, in order that by His death, salvation might be provided for all. If, therefore, they would have recognized and accepted their Messiah, they would not have delivered Him to death, and the whole plan of redemption would have come to naught. To redeem the world, God made it impossible for the nation to receive their Messiah at His first coming.

BLINDED EYES

This was a mystery, that God should set aside His chosen nation (Romans 11:25) in order to redeem His chosen Bride, so that in the end He might be the Redeemer of both. It could not be otherwise, for God had already said in scores of prophetic utterances that the Messiah would be rejected. If then they had received Him, God's word would have been proven false. If this is hard for you to receive, then let me clinch it with Scripture. Then if you still disagree, you can take it up with the Author of the Bible. The Lord Jesus Himself stated this very clearly in John 12. We read that Jesus was foretelling His rejection and death and He says: "And I, if I be lifted up from the earth, will draw all men unto me. This he said, signifying what death he should die" (John 12:32, 33).

He foretold His own death by crucifixion. If it did not happen, Jesus would be proven wrong. However, the people could not believe that the Messiah would be crucified. They had been taught He would set up the Kingdom, and so: "The people answered him, We have heard out of the law [the Scriptures] that Christ abideth for ever: and how sayest thou, The Son of man must be lifted up? . . ." (John 12:34).

This they could not understand. It was a mystery. And why? In order that they might reject Him and God's plan be carried out. Listen, therefore, to these words: "But though he had done so many miracles before them, yet they believed not on him" (John 12:37).

AND WHY NOT?

Why didn't they believe? The answer is unmistakable:

That the saying of Esaias the prophet might be fulfilled, which he spake, Lord, who hath believed our report? and to whom hath the arm of the Lord been revealed?
Therefore *they could not believe* . . . (John 12:38, 39).

Notice those words — *therefore they could not believe,* because Isaiah said they *would not,* and so the verse in its entirety reads:

Therefore they could not believe, because that Esaias said again,
He [God] hath blinded their eyes, and hardened their heart; that they should not see with their eyes, nor understand with their heart, and be converted, and I should heal them.

> These things said Esaias, when he saw his glory, and spake of him (John 12:39-41).

This is the mystery of Israel's rejection of their Messiah. Their eyes were blinded and that blindness continues even today, for Paul says:

> For I would not, brethren, that ye should be ignorant of this mystery, lest ye should be wise in your own conceits; that blindness in part is happened to Israel, until the fulness of the Gentiles be come in (Romans 11:25).

Here is the mystery. God in sovereign wisdom set aside the Nation of Israel, in order that their rejection might be the means of salvation for you and me. The Nation of Israel was judicially blinded by God, but today anyone, whether Jew or Gentile, can *know* the truth, for the mystery has been solved. Here it is: "For God so loved the world, that he gave his only begotten Son, that *whosoever* believeth in him should not perish, but have everlasting life" (John 3:16).

There is no excuse today!

Chapter Seven

THE GREAT DISAPPOINTMENT

But we speak the wisdom of God in a mystery, even the hidden wisdom, which God ordained before the world unto our glory:

Which none of the princes of this world knew: for had they known it, they would not have crucified the Lord of glory.

But as it is written, Eye hath not seen, nor ear heard, neither have entered into the heart of man, the things which God hath prepared for them that love him.

But God hath revealed them unto us by his Spirit: for the Spirit searcheth all things, yea, the deep things of God (I Corinthians 2:7-10).

We must make a clear distinction between the literal Kingdom of Heaven when Jesus personally reigns on earth, and the "mystery of the kingdom of heaven" which refers to God's hidden secret program for the Church during this age while the Kingdom of Heaven itself is postponed. The Kingdom of Heaven was no mystery, but the present age of the Church was not revealed until after Pentecost. For this reason the Lord Jesus Christ was a tremendous, frustrating disappointment to His disciples and many of His followers when He came nineteen hundred years ago. They had confidently expected that when the Messiah came, He would come in the pomp and splendor of a conqueror and deliverer, and His death on the cross was a bitter disappointment. They were looking for a King who would in due time declare Himself, organize His army, rebel against the Roman occupation troops, throw off Caesar's yoke, and set up the glorious Davidic Messianic Kingdom, so voluminously and clearly prophesied by all the seers of old. The Scriptures were replete with prophecies concerning Messiah's glorious reign, when universal peace would be realized, creation be at rest, and Israel safe in possession of her own land.

51

UNIVERSAL EXPECTATION

This was the universal expectation of the devout Israelite of Jesus' day, based upon the sure promises of the Word. They were all looking for a King — not a rejected teacher who would die on a cross. The wise men who traveled all the way from the East came inquiring, "Where is he that is born King of the Jews?" (Matthew 2:2). When John the Baptist came to announce his cousin, he announced Him not only as a "lamb" but the King, and his message was the message of the Kingdom: ". . . Repent ye: for the kingdom of heaven is at hand" (Matthew 3:2).

The disciples of Jesus were also convinced that Jesus was the promised King who would deliver Israel and set up the Kingdom. That was the only reason why they had followed Him, and when He began to show them that instead of reigning as King, He would die on a cross, many of these disillusioned followers walked no more with Him (John 6:60). Though Jesus tried again and again to tell them of their mistake, and that He was *not* going to the Throne but the Cross, they refused to listen, and stubbornly clung to their conviction that He would presently cast off His disguise and reveal Himself as the conquering Messiah King. Peter even dared to suggest that Jesus was entirely mistaken when He spoke of His rejection. We read: "Then Peter took him, and began to rebuke him, saying, Be it far from thee, Lord: this shall not be unto thee" (Matthew 16:22).

Peter suggests that Jesus had overlooked the fact that all the prophets had foretold His glorious victory and reign. Poor Peter, how much he still had to learn!

LOOKING FOR THE KINGDOM

Peter, however, was not alone in his expectations of Jesus setting up the Kingdom. That conviction was shared by the rest of His disciples. Again and again they come with the question, *When?* When, Lord, are You going to declare Yourself? They were already making plans for their place in this Kingdom. The mother of John and James requested places in the King's cabinet for her two sons (Matthew 20:21). On the Mount of Transfiguration Peter was sure that the moment for the setting up of the Kingdom had come, when Jesus conferred with Moses and Elijah, past deliverers of Israel from physical bondage (Moses) and spiritual bondage (Elijah). He suggested setting up military headquarters right then and there when he said: ". . . let us make here three tabernacles; one for thee, and one for Moses, and one for Elias" (Matthew 17:4).

Even after the death and resurrection of Jesus, they still clung to the hope of the setting up of the literal Kingdom. For forty days Jesus had been instructing the disciples and "speaking of the things pertaining to the kingdom" (Acts 1:3), and here they are now on the Mount of Olives, the very place which the Prophet Zechariah had indicated as the place from which the Messiah King would launch His campaign and set up the Kingdom. Undoubtedly as these eleven were alone on Mount Olivet with Jesus they must have been thinking on the verse: "And his [Messiah's] feet shall stand in that day upon the mount of Olives, which is before Jerusalem on the east . . ." (Zechariah 14:4).

Well, here they are. Here is the King, His feet standing on the Mount of Olives and we do not wonder nor can we censure the disciples for their excited question which burst from their lips: ". . . Lord, wilt thou at *this time* restore again the kingdom to Israel?" (Acts 1:6).

We pause here to point out that if Jesus meant to teach that there would not be a *literal* setting up of the Kingdom, no literal restoration of the Nation of Israel, then here was the place to set His disciples straight on their mistaken hope of a Messianic Millennial Kingdom. If Jesus meant that the prophecies of Israel's restoration must be spiritualized and applied to the Church, if God is all through with Israel nationally, and there is to be no future literal Kingdom on earth, and that all the promises to Israel are fulfilled in the Church, then I declare that here was the place for Jesus to explain that they were mistaken in their hopes of a literal Kingdom. Why didn't He say, You are all mistaken about a literal reign of Messiah on earth? All of the promises of the Kingdom are fulfilled in the calling out of the Church. There is no future national restoration of Israel. Israel today means the Church, and the Church is the Kingdom. I repeat, if that is so, then why did not Jesus dispel the notion of the disciples when they asked eagerly: "Lord, wilt thou at this time restore again the kingdom to Israel?"

But He did not say, "Forget about a literal kingdom on earth.

Forget about the Throne of David, and the return of the Nation of Israel to the land." Jesus said no such thing, but instead He replies that it *will come*, but the exact time is not for them to know: "And he said unto them, It is not for you to know the *times* or the seasons, which the Father hath put in his own power" (Acts 1:7).

THE TRAVELERS TO EMMAUS

We mention one other incident to show how deep-seated was the expectation of the Kingdom in the hearts of the disciples. They were looking for Jesus to declare Himself King, and were frustrated and discouraged, surprised and bewildered, when the end came on a cross and in a tomb. On the day of the resurrection two disciples, Cleopas and his partner, were plodding wearily and sadly to their home in Emmaus, some six miles from Jerusalem. The conversation was about their great disappointment. And then Jesus, unrecognized by them, joins them on the way and inquires into the cause of their dejection and deep sadness. In surprise they say, "Where have you been the last few days? Haven't you heard about what they did to Jesus of Nazareth?" And then they give expression to their great disappointment as they say: "But we trusted that it had been he which should have redeemed Israel: and besides all this today is the third day since these things were done" (Luke 24:21).

And then Jesus opened up the Scriptures concerning His death and resurrection first, before the setting up of the Kingdom.

OTHERS SHARED THE VIEW

The disciples, however, were not the only ones who were mistaken in their expectation of a conquering King and disappointed when the end came so ignominiously. The multitudes also had the same expectation. Once when Jesus was approaching Jerusalem the people thought He was going to set up the Kingdom right there. We are told that as He drew nigh unto Jerusalem, ". . . they thought that the kingdom of God should immediately appear" (Luke 19:11).

To set them straight He gave them the parable of the postponed Kingdom (Luke 19:12-27). On another occasion the crowd would have drafted Him, if Jesus had permitted them. We read: "When Jesus therefore perceived that they would come and take him by force, to make him a king, he departed again into a mountain himself alone" (John 6:15).

His Enemies Also

From this we see how deep the conviction that when Messiah came He would come in power, majesty, and glory. He would dash His enemies in pieces. He would declare the decree and assume the Throne of David and rule over the restored Kingdom of Israel. This they confidently expected. They acclaimed Him as the promised Messiah when at His so-called "triumphal" entry into Jerusalem the crowd chanted, ". . . Blessed be the King that cometh in the name of the Lord: peace in heaven, and glory in the highest" (Luke 19:38).

This they believed was the literal fulfillment of the promise of the coming King in Zechariah 9:9.

But even His enemies realized that the prophecies had predicted Messiah as a King, and so they mockingly derided Him when He failed to set up the Kingdom and deliver the Nation of Israel. They gave expression to their deep disappointment by putting a purple robe on Him, placing a mock crown upon His head, and a frail reed for a scepter in His hand. Then they kneeled before Him and cried, "Hail, King of the Jews!" (John 19:3). Over Him on the cross was the contemptuous sign of ridicule, JESUS OF NAZARETH THE KING OF THE JEWS (John 19:19).

Yes, indeed, Jesus was a tragic disappointment, for He ". . . was in the world, and the world was made by him, and the world knew him not. He came unto his own, and his own received him not" (John 1:10, 11).

We would ask the question here, which we hope to answer more fully later on — Why did His people, even His followers, fail to see His rejection and the cross? Certainly the same Old Testament Scripture which told in glowing terms of the glory of His Kingdom had also very clearly foretold His rejection and death. These same prophets had prophesied that He would be "despised and rejected" (Isaiah 53:3). It had predicted His lowly birth, His death on the cross, the piercing of His hands and feet, His awful thirst, even giving the very words He would speak on the cross (Psalm 22). All through the Old Testament His rejection by the nation was foretold and Jesus castigates the disciples on the Emmaus road for their failure to identify them, as He says: ". . . O fools, and slow of heart to believe all that the prophets have spoken: Ought not Christ to have suffered these things, and to enter into his glory?" (Luke 24:25, 26).

Why didn't they see these things? How could they overlook these Scriptures which to us are as plain as day? Do you know the Bible answer? It is one of the deepest mysteries, hidden from the eyes of men until after the death and resurrection of Jesus. It is the *mystery* of the Kingdom of Heaven. It was absolutely necessary and essential that Israel should *not* recognize her Messiah. It was God's plan that they *must* reject Him when He came. For this reason God blinded the eyes of the leaders of the nation, so that in their ignorance they might put their Messiah to death as an indispensable and foreordained means of carrying out God's program for the whole world. This is the *mystery* of the Kingdom of Heaven — hidden from the Nation of Israel — revealed today only to the children of God.

Now if you find difficulty in accepting the dogmatic statement that Israel's crucifixion of their Messiah was a necessity, a part of God's foreordained plan, and it could not have been otherwise, then, before you take issue with those statements, read very carefully Matthew 13:10-13; John 12:37-40; Romans 11:7-12; and Ephesians 3:1-10.

We may in measure excuse Israel, for, says Paul, they did it in ignorance (Acts 3:17). We may in measure excuse those who crucified Christ for, says Paul again, they did not know the mystery of the Kingdom of Heaven, "for had they known it, they would not have crucified the Lord of glory" (I Corinthians 2:8).

But for us there is no excuse. The veil has been lifted and on this side of Pentecost we know that Jesus had to die for our sins, and that He did die for our sins, and rose for our justification. And now the message is clear. It is no mystery any more, "For there is no difference. . . . For whosoever shall call upon the name of the Lord shall be saved" (Romans 10:12, 13).

Chapter Eight

HATH GOD CAST AWAY HIS PEOPLE?

Jesus Christ was a tremendous disappointment when He came the first time. It seems that everyone was disappointed in Him when He failed to deliver the Nation of Israel from their Gentile oppressors. All the prophets had foretold that when Messiah came He would throw off the Roman yoke, assume the Throne of David, bring in the Kingdom of Heaven, and restore the Nation of Israel. Believing this, His disciples had followed Him but when the road led up the hill of Calvary instead, they all forsook Him and fled (Mark 14:50). They had dreamed of the glory and majesty of Messiah's reign. Eagerly they had gone forth proclaiming the message of the Kingdom: ". . . Repent ye: for the kingdom of heaven is at hand" (Matthew 3:2).

Gradually it became apparent that something was wrong somewhere, and the disciples were confused when, instead of the glory of Messiah's throne, the shadow of a cross appeared. It is then that Jesus begins to reveal to them that He was not going to set up His Kingdom at this time, but instead was going to die. This was a great shock and bitter disappointment and as a result we read one of the saddest records in the Bible: "From that time many of his disciples went back, and walked no more with him" (John 6:66).

WHAT WAS WRONG?

But all this was in God's plan. Before the Messiah was to set up the Kingdom He would come first to die for the sins of the whole world. God's plan of redemption included far more than the redemption of one nation Israel — for it embraced all mankind. To accomplish this, God blinded the eyes of the nation until after the sacrifice had been made and then revealed that secret age of grace never before made known. It is called the "dispensation of the grace of God" (Ephesians 3:2); "the mysteries of the kingdom" (Matthew 13:11); the

57

"mystery among the Gentiles" (Colossians 1:27). The "kingdom of heaven" was no mystery, for that had been clearly revealed and the disciples were earnestly expecting our Lord to set up that Kingdom at His first coming. Their confusion resulted from their ignorance of the *mystery of the Kingdom.* This mystery was the secret that at the first coming Jesus would be rejected, the Nation of Israel disowned, and scattered for centuries among the nations, the Kingdom would be postponed, and in the interval the Lord would call out the Church to be His Bride and reign with Him in the Kingdom age of the future.

STILL A MYSTERY

This secret plan was made public after Pentecost and the mystery explained by the Holy Spirit through the apostles and especially Paul. But even though the truth of the setting aside of Israel and the postponement of the Kingdom is so clearly explained, it still is a mystery to great multitudes of people — to literal Israel — and those who call themselves "spiritual Israel." Unless we see the *difference* between God's plan for the Nation of Israel and the program of the Church in this dispensation, we shall remain in darkness and grope about in a dispensational fog. The key to the understanding of prophecy is to recognize this mystery of Israel's temporary rejection. To teach that God is all through with Israel as a nation, that they will never be literally fully restored as a nation to the promised land, to deny the literal reign of Messiah on this earth over the house of Jacob, is to remain in blindness concerning God's program. To teach that we — the Church — are now spiritual Israel, and all the prophecies of Israel's restoration and future blessing must be spiritualized to apply to the Church, is to shut one's self up in darkness concerning God's marvelous plan for both Israel and the Church.

Has the Church taken Israel's place? Is God all done with Israel as a nation to be restored in earthly Kingdom glory? Paul anticipated this question, and asks:

> I say then, Hath God cast away his people? God forbid.
> For I also am an Israelite, of the seed of Abraham, of the
> tribe of Benjamin.
>   God hath not cast away his people which he foreknew
> . . . (Romans 11:1, 2).

We have already seen how God "set aside" the nation for a time, but He has not cast them off for good. This is settled by verse 25 to which we return once again. We make no apologies for repeating it:

> For I would not, brethren, that ye should be ignorant of
> this mystery, lest ye should be wise in your own conceits;
> that blindness in part is happened to Israel, until the fulness of the Gentiles be come in (Romans 11:25).

One fails to understand how anyone can miss the simple message of this verse. Paul says that blindness is happened to Israel *until* the Church is complete. How strange that men should still confuse the Nation of Israel and the Body of Christ, the Church. In talking to one Christian brother who believes his church is spiritual Israel, I referred him to this verse (Romans 11:25) and he replied, "Well, I believe that Israel means the Church." So I substituted the word "church" for "Israel" in this verse and read it "Now I would not, brethren, that ye should be ignorant concerning this mystery, lest ye should be wise in your own conceits; that blindness in part is happened to the *church* (spiritual Israel) until the fulness of the Gentiles be come in." Figure that out! Since blindness is upon Israel, that probably accounts for the blindness of those who claim they now are Israel.

HARD TO GIVE UP

It is passing strange how anyone can fail to see the truth of the mystery when it is so clearly explained. But it was ever thus. After the death and resurrection of Christ and even after Pentecost, the followers of Jesus still did not understand. *Up until* the eighth chapter of Acts, the Gospel was preached exclusively by the apostles to the Jews — to Israel. The message of Peter at Pentecost was still the message of the Kingdom, addressed only to Jews, "Ye men of Israel, hear these words" (Acts 2:22).

> . . . Repent, and be baptized every one of you in the name
> of Jesus Christ for the remission of sins, and ye shall receive the gift of the Holy Ghost (Acts 2:38).

This was still the Kingdom message; that is not the message we are to preach today. Our message today is: "Believe on the Lord Jesus Christ, and thou shalt be saved, and thy house" (Acts 16:31).

Up until the stoning of Stephen it was the Kingdom message and went only to Israel. In Acts 11 we read:

Now they which were scattered abroad upon the persecution that arose about Stephen travelled as far as Phenice, and Cyprus, and Antioch, preaching the word to *none but unto the Jews only* (Acts 11:19).

ENTER PAUL

With the conversion of Paul a new situation arose. After Paul's conversion he received the revelation of the *mystery* and goes out with Barnabas to preach to the Gentiles, a new message of grace. It was not "repent, for the kingdom is at hand," but it was the message of grace — salvation through faith without the deeds of the law. To join the Kingdom Nation one must be circumcised and keep the law, but Paul preached salvation by faith without circumcision or being placed under the law of Moses. This was a new message and soon caused quite a stir. The news reached Jerusalem, and a group of legalists who did not understand the mystery of Israel's rejection and the calling out of the Church traveled to Antioch and began to oppose Paul, and taught: ". . . Except ye be circumcised after the manner of Moses, ye cannot be saved" (Acts 15:1).

This started a riot, and the contention became so hot they decided to go to Jerusalem to report to the apostles. A meeting was called and Paul was accused of teaching heresy — salvation by grace without the law (Acts 15:5). A first-class argument arose (Acts 15:7), which quieted down only when Peter got up and said, "I agree with Paul." He then rehearses how God had sent him to the home of the Gentile Cornelius and saved that group without becoming Jews. Then Paul and Barnabas were called upon and gave their experiences on their missionary journey.

THE BIG QUESTION

A deep silence followed, for this presented a problem — a grave problem. It was this — if God is now saving Gentiles without requiring them to become Jews by circumcision and placing themselves under the laws of Moses, if God is now calling out the Church, then what about all the promises of the coming Kingdom? If God is now forming a body of believers from all nations wholly separate from the Nation of Israel, then is God all done with the nation? Has the Church taken the place of Israel? Has the Church become spiritual Israel, and must all the prophecies of the Kingdom, the restoration of Israel, the fulfillment of the covenant promise to Abraham concerning the land of Canaan as the everlasting inheritance of the seed, must all this be now abandoned and applied to this new body? That was the question, a question which still exists today. There are those who share Israel's blindness, who say, "Yes, the Church has taken Israel's place and all the glowing promises of the glorious kingdom of Israel must be spiritualized and transferred to the Church." The Church is the *kingdom* and poor Israel is left with the curses, while we appropriate the blessings. To all who still hold to this interpretation, I would counsel to read the verdict of this first council in Jerusalem. It was all settled there nineteen hundred years ago and yet the error persists. Listen to James:

> And after they had held their peace, James answered, saying, Men and brethren, hearken unto me:
> Simeon [Peter] hath declared how God at the first did visit the Gentiles, to take out of them a people for his name (Acts 15:13, 14).

The program for this age, while the Church is formed, says James, is not the setting up of the Kingdom or the conversion of the world. Instead, the Lord is *calling out* from among the nations a people for His name. It will be a remnant, a small group, who will comprise the Body and Bride of Christ. The word *church* in the Greek is "ekklesia" meaning "to call out." Not great masses, but here and there a minority are "called out."

"Now this," says James, "is not contrary to the Kingdom promises." The Church is not the Kingdom. This calling out of the Church does not take the place of the Kingdom, but is an entirely separate thing, which has been a mystery hidden until now, and this is not contrary to the Scriptures, and so James explains the mystery, as he says:

> And to this agree the words of the prophets. . . .
> After this I will return, and will build again the tabernacle of David, which is fallen down; and I will build again the ruins thereof, and I will set it up (Acts 15:15, 16).

AFTER THIS

After this I will return. After what? After He has called out "a people for his name." Then He will return. After the Church is complete, after the fulness of the Gentiles be come in, then I will return and restore the glory of the Davidic Kingdom. The tabernacle of David, the glorious Kingdom will be restored. And then follows the great revival, for James adds:

> That the residue of men might seek after the Lord, and all the Gentiles, upon whom my name is called, saith the Lord, who doeth all these things.
> Known unto God are all his works from the beginning of the world (Acts 15:17, 18).

Here then is the revelation of the mystery of the Kingdom of Heaven. First Jesus came to be rejected and crucified. Israel is set aside as a nation, and the Church is being called out. When the number of the elect is full, the Lord will take out His Bride at the Rapture, God will begin to deal again with Israel in the Tribulation, and Jesus will come to deliver the nation, re-establish them in their land, and fulfill every covenant promise to literal Israel. This is the message the world needs today.

Today God is calling out those who believe, that they may share in the glory of His Second Coming. The time is near. Israel is already gathering in the land as a token of her ultimate restoration, and the next event on the program seems to be the shout from the air, and Jesus shall come. Will you be among those who will be caught away before the judgment of God falls upon this world? You can settle it right now. "Believe on the Lord Jesus Christ, and thou shalt be saved . . ." (Acts 16:31).

Chapter Nine

BLIND EYES AND DEAF EARS

And he said, Go, and tell this people, Hear ye indeed, but understand not; and see ye indeed, but perceive not.

Make the heart of this people fat, and make their ears heavy, and shut their eyes; lest they see with their eyes, and hear with their ears, and understand with their heart, and convert, and be healed (Isaiah 6: 9, 10).

This is one of the strangest commissions ever given to man. Isaiah the Prophet of the Lord is commissioned by God to go and preach to a nation the message God would give to him. But the Lord tells the prophet beforehand that the people will not believe him at all, but will reject his message. Yet he is ordered to preach anyway, even though it will result in closing their eyes and ears. God Himself will see to it that they will not understand the message, for God says through Paul:

What then? Israel hath not obtained that which he seeketh for; but the election hath obtained it, and the rest were blinded

(According as it is written, God hath given them [Israel] the spirit of slumber, eyes that they should not see, and ears that they should not hear;) unto this day (Romans 11:7, 8).

When Jesus came there was a remnant, a small minority who recognized Him and owned Him as Saviour. These are called a "remnant according to the election of grace" (Romans 11:5). But the rest, the nation, through its leaders were blinded by God in order that they should not recognize their Messiah. This had to be so, for God had foretold that it would be so when He inspired the prophets to write: "God hath blinded their eyes."

ADDED EVIDENCE

Paul then continues to quote from the Psalms to prove that
the blinding of Israel was in God's foreknown plan:

> And David saith, Let their table be made a snare, and a
> trap, and a stumblingblock, and a recompence unto them
> [Israel]:
> Let their eyes be darkened, that they may not see, and
> bow down their back alway (Romans 11:9, 10).

This indeed is a mystery. The Messiah came, offered the
Kingdom to Israel in good faith, but they rejected His offer
and crucified the Prince of Life, and as a result God cast them
off, drove them out of the land, allowed the city of Jerusalem
to be sacked, and scattered the nation for nineteen hundred
years among the Gentiles. All that is history. But here is the
puzzle. This rejection of their Messiah had been foretold.
The setting aside of the nation had also been abundantly foretold. It was part of God's plan, and so it had to happen. Israel
must reject her Messiah if God's Word is to be true. Suppose
Israel had received her Messiah — then what about all the
prophecies written centuries before? They would have been
proven false and God's Word untrue. We make no apologies for
repeating the record of John. It is so important it can bear repeating, so we refer to it again:

> But though he [Jesus] had done so many miracles before
> them, yet they believed not on him:
> That the saying of Esaias the prophet might be fulfilled,
> which he spake, Lord, who hath believed our report? and
> to whom hath the arm of the Lord been revealed?
> *Therefore they could not believe*, because that Esaias
> said again,
> He [God] hath blinded their eyes, and hardened their
> heart; that they should not see with their eyes, nor under-
> stand with their heart, and be converted, and I should heal
> them (John 12:37-40).

There you have it! That is the Word of God, and you can
take it or leave it. Do you find this hard to believe? Unless
you know *why* God blinded their eyes and hardened their
hearts, it is indeed hard to accept. Is God arbitrary in His
dealings? Is there unrighteousness with God? Is He a God of
caprice? How thankful we are that God Himself gives us the
answer through the Apostle Paul. The question was already

raised by Paul: "I say then, Have they stumbled that they should fall? . . ." (Romans 11:11).

Did God for no reason at all place a stumblingblock in their way, just to see them fall? The very suggestion shocked the apostle, and he hurries to say: ". . . God forbid: but rather through their fall salvation is come unto the Gentiles, for to provoke them to jealousy" (Romans 11:11).

Think of that! Through the fall of Israel, salvation is made possible for the Gentiles. To be a Saviour, Christ must die, and someone must be responsible for His death. God, therefore, chose the Nation of Israel to be the instrument of Christ's death and sacrifice that salvation might come to the whole world. God, according to His eternal counsel, chose the Nation of Israel to be sacrificed for us. God not only gave His Son Jesus Christ to die for us, but He rejected His own chosen people and sacrificed them, that we might share in salvation. This is the Great Mystery. This is the meaning of that tremendous statement:

". . . THROUGH THEIR [ISRAEL'S] FALL SALVATION IS COME UNTO THE GENTILES . . ." (Romans 11:11).

This was the mystery not understood in other ages, that when Messiah came the first time He would be rejected by His own, He would go to the cross, Israel would be rejected and scattered among the nations, while God was carrying out His hidden plan (hidden before) in calling out the Church — the Body of Christ — and then *after that* He would return and set up the Kingdom of Heaven on earth, for one thousand blessed years.

ISRAEL'S RESTORATION

Israel is not cast off forever. God has not abandoned the nation, and the Church is not now Israel. God is not yet through with them, but is going to reward them abundantly in the future. After the Church Age is finished, then their Messiah will come again, restore the nation to the former glory in Palestine, and settle them forever in the land. This Paul now affirms, "Now if the fall of them [Israel] be the riches of the world, and the diminishing of them the riches of the Gentiles; how much more their fulness?" (Romans 11:12).

This was the mystery of the Kingdom of Heaven. We might express it as the mystery "concerning" the Kingdom of Heaven, or the hidden aspect of the Kingdom. The Old Testament saints believed when Messiah came He would set up the Kingdom.

They could not understand how He could both suffer and be glorified. They did not know there was an interval, an hiatus between the suffering and the glory. The dispersion of Israel, the temporary setting aside of the nation, the postponement of the Kingdom, the calling out of the Church — all this was a mystery.

No Surprise to God

However, this was all according to plan. God had so ordered it from eternity, and therefore, all the prophets had foretold it. God planned it all. This is stated over and over again. Jesus knew this. He said, "And as Moses lifted up the serpent in the wilderness, even so *must* the Son of man be lifted up" (John 3:14).

Or listen to Peter on the day of Pentecost as he addresses the Jews at Jerusalem:

> Ye men of Israel, hear these words; Jesus of Nazareth, a man approved of God among you by miracles and wonders and signs, which God did by him in the midst of you, as ye yourselves also know:
>
> Him, being delivered by the *determinate counsel* and *foreknowledge of God,* ye have taken, and by wicked hands have crucified and slain (Acts 2:22, 23).

Peter says that the crucifixion of Jesus at the hands of Israel was according to the *determinate counsel and foreknowledge of God.* We repeat, therefore, the Mystery of the Kingdom of Heaven was this present Church age, during which the Kingdom nation is set aside, the Kingdom postponed until the Bride of Christ is complete, and then the Messiah will return, restore the Kingdom to Israel, and all the prophecies will be fulfilled and the Kingdom of Heaven — the reign of Heaven's King on earth will be realized. The Kingdom of Heaven is the literal Kingdom of Christ on earth. The mystery is the postponement of the Kingdom and the calling out of the Church.

Secret From Beginning

This mystery was kept secret since the world began (Romans 16:25), "But now is made manifest, and by the scriptures of the prophets . . . made known to all nations for the obedience of faith" (Romans 16:26).

In Colossians, Paul speaking of his ministry of the Gospel to the Church calls it,

. . . the mystery which hath been hid from ages and from generations, but now is made manifest to his saints:

To whom God would make known what is the riches of the glory of this mystery among the Gentiles; which is Christ in you, the hope of glory (Colossians 1:26, 27).

In order that this Gospel of the grace of God might be made manifest to all the world, the Lord set aside and rejected the Nation of Israel and permitted them to crucify their Messiah, that we by His death might be saved.

No Excuse for Ignorance

This was the secret in other ages, but it is a secret no longer. The mystery is cleared up and Paul says,

For I would not, brethren, that ye should be ignorant of this mystery, lest ye should be wise in your own conceits; that blindness in part is happened to Israel, *until* the fulness of the Gentiles be come in.

And so all Israel shall be saved: as it is written, There shall come out of Sion the Deliverer, and shall turn away ungodliness from Jacob:

For this is my covenant unto them, when I shall take away their sins (Romans 11:25-27).

It is a secret no longer. There is no excuse any more. During this dispensation national blindness rests upon Israel *until* the fulness of the Gentiles be come in. When the Church is complete, then Christ will take her out, begin to deal again with Israel, and set up the Kingdom upon earth.

Today blindness is upon them, and Paul asserts:

As concerning the gospel, they are enemies for your sakes: but as touching the election, they are beloved for the fathers' sakes.

For the gifts and calling of God are without repentance (Romans 11:28, 29).

God has not forgotten Israel. God hath not cast away His people. He will remember His covenant and will keep His promise of the Kingdom. But in order that we might be saved, their eyes have been blinded. Listen to the unmistakable words of Paul:

For as ye in times past have not believed God, yet have now obtained mercy through their unbelief:

Even so have these also now not believed, that through your mercy they also may obtain mercy.

> For God hath concluded them all in unbelief, that he
> might have mercy upon all (Romans 11:30-32).

This revelation staggered Paul as it staggers us. To think that
God would reject His chosen people Israel in order to save the
Gentiles, and then later redeem Israel as a nation, also caused
Paul to cry out in wonder and adoration:

> O the depth of the riches both of the wisdom and knowl-
> edge of God! how unsearchable are his judgments, and
> his ways past finding out!
> For who hath known the mind of the Lord? or who
> hath been his counsellor?
> Or who hath first given to him, and it shall be recom-
> pensed unto him again?
> For of him, and through him, and to him, are all things:
> to whom be glory for ever. Amen (Romans 11:33-36).

Chapter Ten

THE NEW MESSAGE OF JESUS

The rejection of the Messiah by the Nation of Israel was inevitable and predetermined by God. It was part of God's plan, His over-all plan of redemption. All the prophets had foretold the rejection of the King, and therefore, it had to come to pass or the prophecies given beforehand would be proved false. The death of Christ at the hands of Israel was no surprise to God. Peter in addressing Israel on Pentecost says concerning Jesus: "Him, being delivered by the determinate counsel and foreknowledge of God, ye have taken, and by wicked hands have crucified . . ." (Acts 2:23).

In Peter's second sermon he repeats this truth. He says to the Jews:

And now, brethren, I wot that through ignorance ye did it. . . .
But those things, which God before had shewed . . . that Christ should suffer, he hath so fulfilled (Acts 3: 17, 18).

Ignorance caused the Jews to crucify Christ, and Jesus prayed, "Father, forgive them; for they know not what they do" (Luke 23:34). This ignorance was God-inflicted blindness. Jesus deliberately spoke in such a way that the Jews would *not* understand His message. This was the reason Jesus spake in parables, in order that the truth might remain hidden, except to those to whom it would be supernaturally revealed.

When I was a child in Sunday school I was taught that a parable is "an earthly story with a heavenly meaning." In other words, a parable was an illustration to illuminate some spiritual truth. But this definition is only partly true and mostly wrong. The Bible presents quite a different picture of a parable and tells us that it was a method of teaching designed to "veil" and "hide" the truth rather than reveal it, except to those to whom the truth is supernaturally revealed. Parables are revelations of mysteries which only certain favored ones were able

69

to understand. David in Psalm 78 says about a parable, "I will utter *dark* sayings of old."

When Jesus, therefore, began teaching by parables in Matthew 13, even His disciples were confused until He Himself gave the interpretation. And so they asked Him: ". . . Why speakest thou unto them in parables?" (Matthew 13:10).

Up until the thirteenth chapter of Matthew Jesus had not taught in parables, but His message was plain, clear, direct, and easily understandable. It was the offer of Himself and the Kingdom to the people of Israel, upon condition of faith in His Messiahship and repentance of their sins. The message was unmistakable. He had come as the King of Israel to restore the kingdom of David and deliver the nation from the yoke of the Gentiles. The first twelve chapters of Matthew are a graphic portrayal of this kingly offer. In Matthew chapter 1 we have His claim to the Kingdom. It contains the genealogy of Jesus from Abraham (father of the nation) through David and Solomon up to Joseph, the foster father of Jesus. Then follows the record of His birth in the kingly line of Joseph and Mary. This established His claim as the Son of David and Messiah of Israel.

HIS RECEPTION

In Matthew 2 we have the royal reception of the King. The wise men from the east came to do homage to the King. Their question was, "Where is he that is born King of the Jews?" (Matthew 2:2). They worshiped him (thereby acknowledging His deity) and then presented Him with regal presents, "gold, frankincense, and myrrh." It was a reception fit for a King. And in passing, will you notice the entirely different account in Luke? Here poor shepherds found a Baby in swaddling clothes, lying in a manger in a stable. This was entirely in keeping with Luke, for in Luke Jesus is the "Son of man," the human Saviour who "came to seek and to save that which was lost" (Luke 19:10). No mention here of costly gifts, but simply adoration and praise.

THE HERALD OF THE KING

The King's coming must be officially announced by the "court herald" and so before the King presents Himself to His subjects He is preceded and announced by John the Baptist, the King's herald, according to Isaiah: "The voice of him that crieth in the wilderness, *Prepare ye the way of the Lord . . .*" (Isaiah 40:3).

This is in chapter 3 of Matthew. A potentate must be announced, and so it was at His first coming, and so it will be before His Second Coming when Elijah will come to announce the return of Israel's rejected King (Malachi 4:2; Revelation 11:6). Then the King having been officially announced, He sets out to prove that He is fit to be a King by His victory over the enemy. And so Matthew chapter 4 records the preparation of the King by His victory over Satan in His temptation in the wilderness. He proves that He is *able* to lead the nation to victory. He meets the enemy, conquers him, and returns victorious to present His claims to His oppressed people.

THE KING'S CABINET

Before the King begins His reign, He must choose His cabinet of officers who are to carry out His program. This is also recorded in Matthew 4. He begins to call out a company of men, Peter and Andrew, James and John, and later eight more, to whom would be committed the official offer of the Kingdom to the Nation of Israel.

THE CONSTITUTION

But before sending them out, the King gives them the "constitution," the laws and platform of the Kingdom. This is contained in Matthew chapters 5 to 7, known commonly as the Sermon on the Mount. It is the Constitution of the Kingdom which would have prevailed had Israel accepted the King, and is a description of the conditions which shall prevail when Jesus comes again to set up the Kingdom, rejected by Israel the first time.

One more thing must be taken care of before the King sends His officers out to make the proclamation offer of His reign to Israel. He therefore presents His credentials in Matthew chapters 8 and 9, two chapters containing a rapid-fire uninterrupted record of miracles, signs, wonders, and supernatural works to prove His power and authority. In these chapters (Matthew 8 and 9) He heals a leper, a centurion's servant, Peter's mother-in-law, stills the storm, casts out demons, restores a palsied man, cures a woman of an issue of blood, raises a little girl from death, gives sight to the blind, and casts out demons. What more could He do to prove His identity as the promised Messiah and King? He is now ready to make the official offer to the nation, and so we read:

> And when he had called unto him his twelve disciples, he gave them power against unclean spirits, to cast them out, and to heal all manner of sickness and all manner of disease (Matthew 10:1).

These were "kingdom" signs to prove their authority. Then after naming the twelve disciples the King commands the disciples to bring this offer to none but the Nation of Israel.

> These twelve Jesus sent forth, and commanded them, saying, *Go not* into the way of the Gentiles, and into any city of the Samaritans enter ye not:
>   But go rather to the lost sheep of the house of Israel (Matthew 10:5, 6).

The commission Jesus gave His disciples was exclusively for a limited group only. It was not to be preached to any except the Nation of Israel. It is to be the Kingdom message to national Israel. To apply this commission to the Gospel of grace for all the world is to totally destroy the very message Jesus gave to His disciples. We remind you, therefore, that this commission of Jesus to His twelve apostles is not the personal offer of salvation to "whosoever believeth" but was to be limited to the Nation of Israel. The meaning is clear, "*Go not* into the way of the Gentiles."

Then follows the message. It is not the message of the Gospel for all the world — "Believe on the Lord Jesus Christ, and thou shalt be saved" (Acts 16:31), *but* instead it was, "The kingdom of heaven is at hand." It was still the same message John the Baptist, the herald of the King, had preached: ". . . Repent ye: for the kingdom of heaven is at hand" (Matthew 3:2). He does not say the Kingdom of Heaven is here. That would only come if they received their King. Until the King is accepted by them, the Kingdom will not come. And so the message is in the form of an offer, "The kingdom of God is come *nigh* unto you" (Luke 10:9), and again, "The kingdom of heaven is at hand" (Matthew 10:7).

THE KING REJECTED

The message of the Kingdom offer was accompanied by Kingdom signs and Jesus says to them: "Heal the sick, cleanse the lepers, raise the dead, cast out devils: freely ye have received, freely give" (Matthew 10:8).

Now we come to a turning point in the story. After all the evidence of His identity and authority, the nation did not receive the King, but instead in their blindness rejected Him, turned their backs upon Him, and finally succeeded in crucifying Him. "He came unto his own, and his own received him not" (John 1:11).

Matthew 11 and 12, therefore, tell us how the message of the King was received. Chapter 11 opens with the information that the herald of the King, John the Baptist, had been cast in prison. This indicated how the message of the King was being received. Jesus, therefore, begins to upbraid the leaders of the nation for their refusal to heed Him, and begins to reveal His rejection by the nation, and as a result He anticipates His new message for the whole world, and the chapter closes with the well-known invitation: "Come unto me, all ye that labour and are heavy laden, and I will give you rest" (Matthew 11:28).

It is the first hint of the fact that through the rejection of the King by His own nation, the Gospel would eventually go to all the world, and not be limited only to the Nation of Israel. As a result of the rejection of the King, He would go to the cross instead of the throne, and thus obtain salvation for both Jew and Gentile. It is just a pre-glimpse of the hitherto unrevealed plan of God, soon to be made known and taught in the parables of the Kingdom. And so chapter 12 follows with the record of Israel's sin of blasphemy when the Pharisees accuse Jesus of being an emissary of the Devil. They said: ". . . This fellow doth not cast out devils, but by Beelzebub the prince of the devils" (Matthew 12:24).

This was the last straw, and Jesus pronounces judgment upon them:

Wherefore I say unto you, All manner of sin and blasphemy shall be forgiven unto men: but the blasphemy against the Holy Ghost shall not be forgiven unto men.
. . . neither in this world [age], neither in the world [age] to come (Matthew 12:31, 32).

The chapter closes with Jesus' denunciation of the rebellious leaders of the nation, and now we come to an all-important change in the message of Jesus. Having been rejected, He now turns from the nation, and the message of the Kingdom gives way to the message of the mystery of the Kingdom. Notice, therefore, the significant way in which Matthew 13 (the pivotal chapter in the gospel) opens: "The same day went Jesus out of the *house,* and sat by the *sea side*" (Matthew 13:1).

He left the house and He went to the seaside. It is a picture of Jesus leaving the "house of Israel" and now bringing the new message to the whole world. The sea in Scripture is symbolic of the nations of the world. John describes the waters as "peoples, and multitudes, and nations, and tongues" (Revelation 17:15).

BEGINNING OF PARABLES

It is now that Jesus for the first time in His ministry resorts to the use of parables. The first time the word "parable" occurs is in this verse: "And he spake many things unto them in parables . . ." (Matthew 13:3).

Up until now He had spoken plainly, but now He clothes His message in deep mystery. He is now to reveal the mystery of God's hidden plan of salvation for all the world to a select company only. At first the disciples were confused and came to Him in amazement and said: ". . . Why speakest thou unto them in parables?" (Matthew 13:10).

Then Jesus gives us the most amazing answer. He says: ". . . Because it is given unto you to know the mysteries of the kingdom of heaven, but to them it is not given" (Matthew 13:11).

In the coming chapters we shall take up in detail Jesus' teaching concerning the parables and mysteries of the Kingdom, but before we close this section we want to once more point out that Jesus deliberately used parables in order that only those whose spiritual eyes were opened could understand what He meant, but to others it would remain a mystery. Jesus deliberately spoke in such a way that the truth would remain completely hidden from their eyes. Before we can understand the "mysteries" of God, our spiritual eyes, too, must be opened. Until then it will be foolishness. Paul says,

> But the natural man receiveth not the things of the Spirit of God: for they are foolishness unto him: neither can he know them, because they are spiritually discerned (I Corinthians 2:14).

Jesus said, "Except a man be born again, he cannot see" (John 3:3). If you are to understand the parables and mysteries of the Gospel you must first be "born again." This is the first and most important condition. And you may have that experience by simply trusting Jesus Christ as your personal Saviour and believing that He died and rose to save you.

Come to Him in your helplessness and you will experience a mysterious transformation, as wonderful as the receiving of sight by the blind. "Believe on the Lord Jesus Christ, and thou shalt be saved . . ." (Acts 16:31).

Chapter Eleven

WHY JESUS HID HIMSELF

If the Nation of Israel had received Christ and owned Him as their Messiah and King when He came nineteen hundred years ago, He would not have gone to the cross. There would have been no Calvary, and no empty tomb. There would have been no atonement for sin, no salvation to offer to a lost world. It was therefore indispensably necessary for Jesus to be rejected by the nation. It could not have been otherwise, for God had so planned it from eternity and the prophets had so foretold it. Jesus must be rejected according to the fore-ordained program of God. And so, while the offer to Israel was made in good faith, God also foreknew that Jesus would not be received. In fact, God saw to it that His purpose in the death of Jesus should be accomplished, for Acts 4:28 says that Jesus was slain according to the counsel "determined before to be done."

According to this plan we saw that Jesus came as a King, offered Himself as a King, but was rejected. And then being rejected, He turned from them and begins to proclaim a new and different message. This new message was clothed in deep mystery and shrouded in a veil of parabolic teaching. In Matthew 13, after the leaders of Israel had refused to own Christ as Messiah, Jesus resorts to a unique method of teaching designed to effectively blind the eyes of His rejectors. He begins to teach in parables. The disciples came to Jesus and asked in their confusion: ". . . Why speakest thou unto them in parables?" (Matthew 13:10).

The answer of Jesus is revolutionary and significant. He says, in essence, "a parable is not designed to reveal truth, but to conceal it, lest men should believe it." If this startles you, then follow the teaching of the Saviour:

> He answered and said unto them, *Because* it is given unto you to know the mysteries of the kingdom of heaven, but to them [the leaders of the nation] it is not given (Matthew 13:11).

Jesus is about to reveal a new truth, hidden up until this time. But this truth was to be revealed only to His followers; to all others it must remain a secret. And so Jesus calls this new revelation a "mystery." He calls it specifically the "mysteries of the kingdom of heaven."

Now the truth concerning the future Kingdom upon this earth was no mystery to the Old Testament saints. It had been abundantly prophesied by all the writers of the Old Testament, beginning with Moses and ending with Malachi. As a result the people expected that when Messiah came He would immediately set up this Kingdom. The disciples expected this and asked Him repeatedly about it. Even after the resurrection they inquired, ". . . Lord, wilt thou at this time restore again the kingdom to Israel?" (Acts 1:6).

Even John the Baptist believed this and became greatly confused, when instead of the Throne, the cross came into view. In his confusion in prison he sent his disciples to ask whether Jesus was really the One whom He had confidently announced. The disciples of Jesus had no doubt about the Kingdom and expected momentarily that Jesus would declare Himself and deliver Israel. So confident were they of this that they were already picking their places in the Kingdom.

And then came the surprise and the disappointment. Instead of being accepted as King, He had been rejected. The reason for all this misunderstanding was their ignorance concerning the "mystery form of the Kingdom." They did not see that at His first coming Jesus would be rejected and go back to Heaven, to return at a later time to set up the Kingdom on earth. Between this first coming of Christ and His Second Coming lay an age of mystery. It was the "church age," the "dispensation of grace," during which the King would call out a Bride to sit on His Throne in the Kingdom. This intervening age was not seen or understood by the prophets of old, nor by the disciples. It was the mystery which God did not see fit to reveal until after the rejection of the King.

The mystery was that Christ would not only come to redeem Israel, but by His death also become the Redeemer of the world, and then after that He would set up the Kingdom. The "mystery of the kingdom of heaven" refers then to this present dispensation; while Jesus is in Heaven, Israel is dispersed, and the Church is being called out. It is called a mystery because it was unknown before and also because it is still a mystery to all but believers in the Lord Jesus Christ.

Now to return to Matthew 13. After the rejection of the Messiah, He now prepares to reveal His hidden plan to His disciples. But while revealing it to His own, He must hide it from His enemies. And to accomplish this He resorts to the use of parables. While Jesus explains the parables to His followers, they remain dark and meaningless mysteries to the others. In the eternal purpose and counsels of God, Jesus was to be rejected and slain as a sacrifice for sinners. To accomplish this God must prevent the rulers of Israel from recognizing Him, lest they should accept Him and the cross be by-passed. And to accomplish this Jesus clothes His words in mystery. This is what He says:

> Therefore speak I to them in parables: because they seeing see not; and hearing they hear not, neither do they understand.
>
> And in them is fulfilled the prophecy of Esaias, which saith, By hearing ye shall hear, and shall not understand; and seeing ye shall see, and shall not perceive:
>
> For this people's heart is waxed gross, and their ears are dull of hearing, and their eyes they have closed; lest at any time they should see with their eyes and hear with their ears, and should understand with their heart, and should be converted, and I should heal them (Matthew 13:13-15).

All this Jesus gives as His reason for speaking to them in parables. If they should have understood and been converted then Isaiah's prophecy would have proved false and God's Word been made ineffective. The prophets had all said that the King would be rejected and it had to come to pass. To accomplish this, the eyes of the rulers of Israel were blinded, and Jesus' use of parables assured this blindness.

Does this sound startling and arbitrary? Then remember God is sovereign and infinite in wisdom and has a reason for every act. In Matthew 13:34 the writer tells us:

> All these things spake Jesus unto the multitude in parables; and without a parable spake he not unto them:
>
> That it might be fulfilled which was spoken by the prophet, saying, I will open my mouth in parables; I will utter things which have been kept secret from the foundation of the world (Matthew 13:34, 35).

Jesus did not explain the parables to the crowd, but only when alone with His disciples. Plainly Matthew records:

Then Jesus sent the multitude away, and went into the house: and his disciples came unto him, saying, Declare unto us the parable of the tares of the field (Matthew 13:36).

It is privately with His disciples that Jesus then reveals God's mysterious plan. The King will be rejected and die, the Kingdom postponed, while the Church is gathered out, and then He will return to fulfill every Kingdom promise. But to all the rest the mystery remains. How can the Christ die and still be King? That was the puzzle. When Jesus announced His death to the people they were puzzled. How could Messiah the King die? In John 12:34 the people openly expressed their confusion and bewilderment. They said:

. . . We have heard out of the law that Christ [Messiah] abideth for ever: and how sayest thou, The Son of man must be lifted up? who is this Son of man? (John 12:34).

They failed to recognize Jesus as their Messiah in order that God's purpose, foretold by all the prophets, might be carried out. And so Jesus answers their question:

While ye have light, believe in the light, that ye may be the children of light. These things spake Jesus, and departed, and did hide himself from them (John 12:36).

Jesus hid Himself from them. They were not to believe on Him in spite of all the evidence of His person and authority. And why did they not believe? I would hesitate to give the reason were it not for the fact that Jesus gives it plainly. We have touched on this passage before, but repeat it again for emphasis:

But though he had done so many miracles before them, yet they believed not on him:
    That the saying of Esaias the prophet might be fulfilled, which he spake, Lord, who hath believed our report? and to whom hath the arm of the Lord been revealed? (John 12:37, 38).

Why did not these to whom Jesus spake, believe on Him? Because God had said they would not, and God's Word must stand, and so Jesus makes this startling statement,

Therefore they *could not believe*, because that Esaias said again,
    He [God] hath blinded their eyes, and hardened their heart; that they should not see with their eyes, nor under-

stand with their heart, and be converted, and I should heal them.

These things said Esaias, when he saw his glory . . . (John 12:39-41).

In order for us to be saved and delivered from Hell, Jesus must go to the cross. He must be rejected by His own nation, that we might be redeemed. What a debt of gratitude we owe to the Nation of Israel who was set aside that we might be brought in. But we owe an even greater debt of gratitude to God for this inscrutable, incomprehensible, infinitely wise plan for our redemption. Surely there is no excuse for us today on this side of Calvary, to hear the Gospel and still to be lost, for the invitation now is for all: "Come unto me, all ye that labour and are heavy laden, and I will give you rest" (Matthew 11:28).

Chapter Twelve

THE WOMAN – THE MEAL – THE LEAVEN

There are seven parables in the thirteenth chapter of Matthew called by Jesus "the mysteries of the kingdom of heaven." They are called mysteries because they had never before been revealed. Matthew tells us plainly:

All these things spake Jesus unto the multitude in parables; and without a parable spake he not unto them:
That it might be fulfilled which was spoken by the prophet, saying, I will open my mouth in parables; I will utter things which have been kept secret from the foundation of the world (Matthew 13:34, 35).

In these seven parables, Christ for the first time makes known a part of God's plan, unseen by the prophets of old. It was the revelation concerning this present dispensation of grace, between the first and Second Coming of the Lord Jesus. In these seven parables we have first a revelation of the character of this present age, and then the course of the age. The seven parables in their order are:

1. The parable of the sower
2. The parable of the tares
3. The parable of the mustard seed
4. The parable of leaven
5. The parable of the hid treasure
6. The parable of the precious pearl
7. The parable of the dragnet

THE SOWER

Probably the most familiar of these parables is the first one, usually referred to as the four kinds of soil. A sower went forth to sow. Some seed fell on the wayside and was devoured by the birds. Some fell on stony ground and soon withered away. Other fell among thorns and was choked before it came to fruitage. And then some fell on good ground and produced thirty-, sixty-, and a hundredfold.

81

Many books have been written on these four kinds of hearers. The seed is the Word of God. The soil is the heart of man. Some hear but do not understand. Some show an emotional reaction but only one-fourth ever produce fruit. The parable is a prophecy of the course of this present dispensation. Jesus teaches that the world will not be converted in this age; neither will all men believe the Gospel, but instead a minority, a little flock, a mere remnant will be saved to become members of the Body of Christ. It silences forever the theory that by the preaching of the Gospel, social reform, education, and understanding, the world will become better and better until all will become Christians and the golden age will come by human effort, before the coming again of Christ. Christianity, true Christianity, never was popular with the masses and never can be. When Christianity is popular with the multitudes it is time to examine this brand of "Christianity" to which the world does not object. During this dispensation truly born-again Christians will be a comparatively small company, despised and misunderstood by the world. World conversion during this age is nowhere taught in the Bible, but instead it teaches that God is taking out from the Gentiles a people for His name (Acts 15:14).

THE TARES

The second parable follows naturally. The first teaches that the world will not be converted during this dispensation, and parable number two gives the reason why this will not be. Here are Jesus' own words:

> . . . The kingdom of heaven is likened unto a man which sowed good seed in his field:
> But while men slept, his enemy came and sowed tares among the wheat, and went his way.
> But when the blade was sprung up, and brought forth fruit, then appeared the tares also (Matthew 13:24-26).

Again Jesus gives the explanation. The sower is the Son of Man, the good seed are believers, and the tares are professing unbelievers. The enemy is the Devil; the harvest is the end of the age. The teaching is the same as the first parable with additional details. In the parable of the four soils the seed is the Word of God; in this parable of the tares the seed is the body of truly born-again believers, those in whom the good seed of the Word fell on good ground. But the Devil has a counterfeit company. He has people who look and act like

Christians and associate with believers but are only false professors and counterfeits. They are called "tares" in this parable.

Tares are so similar to wheat they cannot be distinguished
until the harvest. For this reason they are to be left to grow up
together until the end of the age. The lesson is clear. The
children of God (the seed) are scattered in the field (the world).
But wherever these believers are found, Satan sows the children
of darkness, who profess to be Christians and in outward appearance are so like the true children of God that the angels
only in the end may be trusted to separate them. The parable
of the tares and wheat, therefore, is a picture of professing
Christendom today. Wherever true believers are found, Satan
will also have his counterfeits. Their identity will not become
known until Jesus comes to separate the wheat from the tares.

THE MUSTARD SEED

In the third parable (the mustard seed) this truth is further
expanded and developed. It is brief but rich in teaching:

> . . . The kingdom of heaven is like to a grain of mustard
> seed, which a man took, and sowed in his field:
> Which indeed is the least of all seeds: but when it is
> grown, it is the greatest among herbs, and becometh a tree,
> so that the birds of the air come and lodge in the branches
> thereof (Matthew 13:31, 32).

This unnatural growth of an insignificant herb into a tall tree
is a picture of professing Christendom. A mustard seed is
small, and the plant is comparatively small. But this seed was
an anomaly, for it became a tree, so large that the fowls of
the air rested in its branches. It is the same as the tares among
the wheat. It is a false and spurious development. The fowls of
the air are the wicked professors which find a welcome in the
apostate body of Christendom. It is another illustration of the
fact that a universally popular Christianity is a false Christianity.
Nowhere in the Bible is it taught that in this age the true believers will be a popular group, much less a large group. As
this age progresses, therefore, apostasy and error will increase
until the end.

THE LEAVEN

In the fourth parable (the leaven) we have the natural result
of the presence of false professors in the professing church, as
seen in the tares and the unnatural growth of the mustard seed.

. . . The kingdom of heaven is like unto leaven, which a woman took, and hid in three measures of meal, till the whole was leavened (Matthew 13:33).

This parable is the key to the entire chapter on the "Mysteries of the Kingdom." It is exactly in the center of the seven. Someone has said, "The key to the understanding of the New Testament is the book of Matthew, and the key to Matthew is the thirteenth chapter, and the key to the thirteenth chapter is the parable of the leaven. If the interpretation of this parable is wrong, we will be wrong on the whole program of God for this present age." Before giving what we believe to be the correct interpretation of the words of Jesus, we give the commonly accepted but entirely erroneous explanation. We are told that the "leaven" is the Gospel. The woman is the Church. The three measures of meal represent the world. The Church by preaching the Gospel in the world will finally convert all the world and the whole earth will be leavened and converted to Christianity. And so we are told just to have faith in our efforts to bring in the age of universal peace and prosperity when all the world will be converted.

This interpretation does violence to the rest of Bible revelation concerning the meaning of leaven. Leaven is always symbolic of evil, sin, and corruption. Yeast is a destructive agent, and wherever leaven or yeast is mentioned it always signifies evil and error either in doctrine or in morals. In the Old Testament leaven always is symbolic of evil (Genesis 19:3). In the New Testament it is a picture of doctrinal error, and Jesus warns His disciples against the leaven of the Pharisees and Sadducees (Matthew 16:12). In Mark 8:15 He warns them against the leaven of the Herodians. The leaven of the Pharisees was false profession and outward orthodoxy. The leaven of the Sadducees was liberalism and modernism, denying the supernatural and miraculous. The leaven of the Herodians was worldliness and politics in religion.

MALICE AND WICKEDNESS

But leaven also represents evil and error in a moral sense as well as doctrinal. Paul warns the Corinthians against the leaven of malice and wickedness. Paul agrees with the parable of Jesus and asks: ". . . Know ye not that a little leaven leaveneth the whole lump?" (I Corinthians 5:6).

The occasion was a man who lived with his own father's wife, and this "leaven" of fornication threatened to defile the whole church. And so he admonishes them:

> Purge out therefore the old leaven. . . .
> Therefore let us keep the feast, not with old leaven, neither with the leaven of malice and wickedness; but with the unleavened bread of sincerity and truth (I Corinthians 5:7, 8).

We have gone to all this detail to show that leaven everywhere else in Scripture represents evil and error, doctrinally and morally, and gives us the key to the meaning of the parable of Jesus. This is in harmony with the parable of the tares and the mustard tree. Until the end of this age there will be false professors in the Church, tares among the wheat, and when we come to the last and final parable of the dragnet at the end of the age, it still consists of a mixture of both good and bad fish, which will only be identified and separated when Christ comes in judgment.

THE WOMAN — THE MEAL — THE LEAVEN

The woman in the bad ethical sense symbolizes the false church. The meal (food of the saints) is the truth of the Word of God. The leaven is the corruption of the Word by false teachers. It is the introduction of error and false doctrine, human interpretations, religious creeds and dogmas, traditions and superstitions to the Word of God. It is the adding to the truth of God's Word by human traditions and interpretations. It is the Bible *plus* something; the Bible plus church dogma, worldly programs, human organization, popular compromise. And this process of corruption of the Gospel will continue and increase until the whole realm of Christendom has been invaded; and true Bible Christianity, instead of being a peculiar, separated Body, will be replaced by a compromising, anemic, bloodless body with a dead creed, a great religious society without life. In the end the woman, so minutely described as the scarlet woman of Revelation 17 and 18, will succeed in uniting all religions under one great ecumenical apostate church, leavening the whole lump. Before this final state of the leavening process by the great world church, the Lord will come and take out the true believers, separate the tares from the wheat, sort out the good fish from the bad, and then will follow the judgment of the false church, the woman and her illegitimate children who have corrupted the Gospel of the grace of God.

This leavening process of evil in the Church began soon after Pentecost, and has been going on ever since. It is undetected by the masses, for this leavening is a silent process. But as we approach the end, when the whole lump will be leavened, it becomes more evident. Never before has there been so much error taught and deception practiced. Never before has there been such a lack of separation among believers. Never before has there been such tolerance toward false doctrine, indifference and looseness in morals as today. Never before has there been so much activity in the union of various Christian bodies at the expense of fundamental and vital doctrines.

So thoroughly is the leaven mixed with the meal, and so permeated by the leaven is the lump, that there is only one way to stop the process of corruption — to bake it — and kill the leaven. Before the whole lump becomes sour and putrid the Lord will come and take out His own and then pass the whole corrupted lump of the false professing world church through the fires of the Tribulation and judge the woman who introduced it.

Of this judgment we read in Revelation 17. John sees a woman arrayed in purple and scarlet, having in her hand a cup full of abominations and filthiness. And her name is MYSTERY, BABYLON THE GREAT. Before judgment falls upon her, God issues a final warning to the true believers: ". . . Come out of her, my people . . ." (Revelation 18:4).

Judgment is coming. The end of all things is at hand. To be identified with Satan means doom. Have you received Christ as your personal Saviour so that before judgment falls, you will be safe and secure in His own protection and care?

Chapter Thirteen

A TREASURE AND A PEARL

Again, the kingdom of heaven is like unto treasure hid in a field; the which when a man hath found, he hideth, and for joy thereof goeth and selleth all that he hath, and buyeth that field (Matthew 13:44).

The seven parables of the Kingdom, called the mysteries of the Kingdom of Heaven, are a description of the course of this present age, beginning with the death and resurrection of Jesus until His coming again. It relates for us the history of professing Christendom while the ascended Lord is in Heaven preparing a place for us. During this age the Nation of Israel is set aside, scattered among the nations of the world. The prophets had predicted that when Jesus came the first time He would be rejected by His own and as a result the nation would be judged, the Kingdom postponed until He comes back. Of course, the Kingdom was not postponed as far as God's plan was concerned, but postponed in the minds of men, for the prophets and disciples expected Christ to set up the Kingdom when He came the first time nineteen hundred years ago, because this present Church Age was still a mystery which had been hidden. It was all in God's plan but for some reason it was not before revealed.

This is also the meaning of the hidden treasure in the field. It too was something about which little or nothing was known. But now Jesus in telling His disciples what would happen after His rejection, tells them of a treasure hid in a field and purchased with the field by the glad finder. Before identifying this man, the field and the treasure, we again mention the commonly accepted interpretation which has been held by many without any basis of truth in the Scriptures. We are told that the treasure is Jesus Christ or salvation, the buyer of the field is the sinner. This is contrary to the entire revelation of God's plan of salvation. Jesus tells us the field is the world (Matthew 13:38). The sinner does not seek the treasure of salvation; neither does he buy the world (field), but rather forsakes the world to win Christ. Moreover, the sinner has nothing with which to buy the field, for salvation is free. Salvation is not for sale; Christ cannot be bought, neither is He hidden in the field of the world, nor having found Christ does one hide Him again. The interpretation that the buyer is the sinner, the treasure is salvation to be obtained by purchasing the field, breaks down at every point.

CHRIST IS PURCHASER

The Lord Jesus is the buyer of the treasure and the field. He alone has the price of redeeming that which was lost. The Nation of Israel, God's covenant chosen nation, is the treasure hid in the field. At the very outset of the nation's history, after their deliverance from Egypt, Jehovah declared that Israel was to be unto Him "a peculiar treasure . . . above all people" (Exodus 19:5). In Psalm 135:4 David sings: "For the LORD hath chosen Jacob unto himself, and Israel for his peculiar treasure."

The divine merchant man, the Lord, in order to obtain the field hides the treasure, so that in the end both the field and the treasure may become His own. The Scriptures are clear that the Lord set aside Israel, His treasure, in order that by the crucifixion of their Messiah, He might become the Saviour of the world. While the nation is in exile the Lord is offering His salvation to the world. This redemption by which men are to be saved and Israel redeemed cost the Saviour His own life and blood. It cost His all, but He purchased it at the awful cost of His own blood.

The treasure is hid in the field until the field is purchased. Israel is to be set aside until the fulness of the Gentiles be come in. Paul calls this a mystery, and says concerning it:

> For I would not, brethren, that ye should be ignorant of this mystery, lest ye should be wise in your own conceits; that blindness in part is happened to Israel, until the fulness of the Gentiles be come in.
>
> And so all Israel shall be saved: as it is written, There shall come out of Sion the Deliverer, and shall turn away ungodliness from Jacob (Romans 11:25, 26).

This temporary "hiding" of the treasure was God's way of making salvation possible to all. Listen to the words of Paul, speaking of the "treasure," Israel:

As concerning the gospel, they are enemies for your sakes: but as touching the election, they are beloved for the fathers' sakes.

For as ye [Gentiles] in times past have not believed God, yet have now obtained mercy through their [Israel's] unbelief:

Even so have these [Israel] also now not believed, that through your mercy they also may obtain mercy.

For God hath concluded them all [Israel, the treasure] in unbelief, that he might have mercy upon all (Romans 11:28, 30-32).

This we believe to be the teaching of the hidden treasure. To become the Saviour of the world He was slain by His own, resulting in God's judgment upon them, but in the end will show the wonderful wisdom of God in redeeming Israel as His own, and planting them upon their own land.

And this lesson of the hidden treasure leads us naturally to the next parable of our Lord.

Again, the kingdom of heaven is like unto a merchant man, seeking goodly pearls:

Who, when he found one pearl of great price, went and sold all that he had, and bought it (Matthew 13:45, 46).

Once again we look at the almost universally accepted interpretation. The merchant man, we are asked to believe, is the sinner. The pearl of great price is salvation, and the Lord Jesus. The sinner sells all after diligent search, and pays the purchase price of his redemption. Little needs to be said to show how unscriptural is this view, and we wonder how anyone can be blind to the error of such an application. It is diametrically opposed to the whole doctrine of salvation by grace. The sinner does not seek after salvation, for the Bible plainly states, "There is none that seeketh after God" (Romans 3:11). It is Christ who seeks the sinner and not the sinner Christ (Luke 19:10).

Nor does the sinner purchase his salvation. He has nothing wherewith to pay. He is a pauper and not a wealthy merchant man. It is called a pearl of "great price." The sinner has nothing to pay for salvation. We turn from this unscriptural interpretation as entirely opposed to the grace of God.

THE PRECIOUS PEARL

The pearl is the Church of the Lord Jesus Christ. It is found in the sea which represents all nations (Revelation 17:15). The merchant man is the Lord Jesus. To obtain this precious pearl

He sold all that He had, left Heaven's glory, laid aside the form of God, for our sakes became poor, paid the infinite price of His own blood and so redeemed us for His own. Of this Peter says we —

> . . . were not redeemed with corruptible things, as silver and gold. . . .
> But with the precious blood of Christ, as of a lamb without blemish and without spot (I Peter 1:18, 19).

A pearl is one — a perfect symbol of organic unity. It is the result of a wound in the side of an oyster. A grain of sand or other foreign substance causes an irritation within the shell, and the oyster secretes a substance around the foreign body encasing it and making it harmless. The secretion hardens and is added to, bit by bit, until the beautiful pearl comes from its side. So, too, the Church was formed. Sin was the irritation which Christ took for us. He canceled its power and around the atonement for sin builds His Church, part of His own Body. The Lord Jesus was "bruised for our iniquities and wounded for our transgressions." In perfect harmony with the type of Eve's creation, the Bride of the Second Man or last Adam was also taken from His side. Out of this side flowed blood and water — blood to redeem and water to cleanse. One of these days this pearl will be complete and He will present her unto Himself a glorious Church at the wedding of the Lamb.

THE DRAGNET

One more parable remains to complete the description of the program of this Church Age. It is the parable of the dragnet.

> Again, the kingdom of heaven is like unto a net, that was cast into the sea, and gathered of every kind:
> Which, when it was full, they drew to shore, and sat down, and gathered the good into vessels, but cast the bad away (Matthew 13:47, 48).

Unlike some of the other parables, Jesus immediately gives the interpretation. The net is the gospel net; the fish represent men; the sea is a picture of the nations. Into this gospel net, as it is cast into the sea of the nations, come a great number, both good and bad. It is again a picture of professing Christendom, the organized Church, in which are not only the true children of God, but also many false professors and hypocrites. They are all together in the same net, but will not remain so.

It is again the same lesson as the wheat and the tares, the mustard plant, and the leaven. This parable of the net presents the same picture in the sphere of professing Christendom. This mystery age will see a strange admixture of true and false. Just as the age began with the four kinds of soil, with only a minority of true believers, so it will be in the end of the age. The sea is not converted, but out of it the Lord gathers His own. But until the end of the age we are not to judge the true and false. It is not our business to determine who in the professing Church are genuine believers and only mere pretenders. That both will be there unto the end is definitely taught, for Jesus in explaining the parable of the net says:

> So shall it be at the end of the world: the angels shall come forth, and sever the wicked from among the just,
> And shall cast them into the furnace of fire: there shall be wailing and gnashing of teeth (Matthew 13:49, 50).

During this age there will be deception and false profession and Jesus says:

> Not every one that saith unto me, Lord, Lord, shall enter into the kingdom of heaven; but he that doeth the will of my Father which is in heaven.
> Many will say unto me in that day, Lord, Lord, have we not prophesied in thy name? and in thy name have cast out devils? and in thy name done many wonderful works?
> And then will I profess unto them, I never knew you: depart from me, ye that work iniquity (Matthew 7:21-23).

These will be separated from the true when Jesus comes again. Such then is the teaching of the parables of Jesus in Matthew 13. They are mysteries to all except those whose eyes have been opened to the truth of God. It is God's picture of the sphere of Christian profession in this age, a mingled body of true and false, tares and wheat, leaven and meal, good and bad fish. The professing Church is defiled by formalism, worldliness, false doctrine, tradition, and error of every sort.

But within this visible sphere God sees the true children of the true Kingdom of Heaven, destined to reign with Him in the coming Kingdom of Christ upon earth. In this present program God sees in this great field of the world the redeemed of all ages. He sees Israel dispersed and scattered in the field and will soon restore His "treasure." He sees the "pearl," the true members of the body of Christ, His future Bride, and we believe the net is almost full and soon the separation will take place.

In conclusion then, the most important question is: "Do I belong to Him?" We cannot judge others and must wait till Jesus comes to know the true from the false, but we need not wait till then to know for ourselves that we are saved. Have you ever personally by a definite act of faith received Christ as your Saviour? Do you know for a certainty that you are saved? If not, then now is the time to settle it. Trust His promise and believe. Admit you are a helpless sinner, believe that Jesus died and arose for your salvation, and receive Him by faith upon the authority of Him who said,

> That if thou shalt confess with thy mouth the Lord Jesus, and shalt believe in thine heart that God hath raised him from the dead, thou shalt be saved (Romans 10:9).

Chapter Fourteen

THE COURSE OF THIS AGE

The present dispensation in which we live today is an age of mystery. It was a mystery to the Old Testament prophets who saw the coming of the Messiah of Israel to set up His Kingdom on earth, but they failed to see the intervening age of grace, with the setting aside of Israel and the calling out of the Church of Jesus Christ. This was first announced by Jesus to His disciples in Matthew 13, and later fully developed after Pentecost, through the apostles and especially the Apostle Paul, the apostle to the Gentiles. Concerning this mystery he says that it was:

> . . . the revelation of the mystery, which was kept secret since the world began,
> But now is made manifest, and by the scriptures of the prophets, according to the commandment of the everlasting God, made known to all nations for the obedience of faith (Romans 16:25, 26).

In Matthew 13 Jesus teaches His disciples by the use of the seven parables of the Kingdom the characteristics of this present age of mystery. He begins with the parable of the four soils, teaching us that during this age of gospel preaching all will not be converted, but much of the seed will never take root. The last of the parables shows that this condition will continue during this entire dispensation. At the end both saved and unsaved are found in the net.

THE PROGRESS OF THE AGE

Now we want to look at this same truth from a different angle. We believe that in these seven parables we have a description of the progress of this age in seven periods. It is God's prophetic program for this dispensation. While all the parables describe the general condition of professing Christendom during this entire dispensation, they also represent seven successive periods of Church history. The parable of the four soils points to the apostolic age during the first century. It was the great period of sowing when, by the apostles and especially by Paul, the message was sent throughout the entire civilized world. In Colossians 1:6 we read that this Gospel had been preached in all the world. The result was that everywhere churches had sprung up. What a time of sowing that was! Through the efforts of Paul and his associates, churches had been established in Iconium, Derbe, Lystra, Antioch, Thessalonica, Berea, Corinth, Ephesus and many others besides. It was the age of sowing.

Following this first parable is the parable of the tares among the wheat. It fits especially the second and third centuries of Church history with the introduction of error and evil into the Church and the entrance of the world into the body of believers. This naturally resulted in a corruption of the professing Church and developed into that historic period represented by the mustard seed. Early in the fourth century Constantine the emperor of Rome became a convert to Christianity, after presumably having seen the sign of the cross in the sky. He caused his entire army to be baptized and thus become nominal Christians. Christianity became the state religion of Rome in an unscriptural union of Church and State, the Church dominating and dictating to the State. Thus began one of the most evil periods in Church history. Persecution ceased, the Church was subsidized by the State, Christianity became popular instead of despised, and an artificial outgrowth resulted, while the true believers were few and ignored. This was the great anomalous mustard tree. That which should have remained an insignificant little herb became a mighty tree, in which the fowls of the air nested. Everyone belonged to this Church and soon the false believers took over and began introducing the many errors which have corrupted professing Christendom.

THE LEAVEN

Following, therefore, in perfect order this false expansion of Christendom as illustrated in the mustard seed, we come next to that period of Church history described as a woman taking leaven and adding it to three measures of meal until the whole was leavened. The woman is the "world church" of the middle ages, historically referred to as the "dark ages." It was in this period that the leaven of malice, wickedness, formalism, ritualism, and worldliness did its permeating work until it seemed that the truth of the Gospel of the grace of God would be lost entirely. And then came the Renaissance and the days of the Reformation and Counter-Reformation. The true believers in the world were revived, and the light of the Gospel was rekindled by the Reformers.

TREASURE AND PEARL

This great spiritual awakening, following the dark ages of the leavening of the Gospel, brought into light two great truths which had been almost entirely forgotten. These were: (1) The future of the Nation of Israel; and (2) The true nature of the Church of Jesus Christ, as a body of believers and not merely a religious organization. And so following the parable of the leaven we have the parables of the hidden treasure and the precious pearl. The rediscovery of the great truth of Justification by Faith was the key to the identification of the treasure. Israel (God's peculiar treasure) had been lost sight of entirely and the teaching that the Church had taken Israel's place was universally believed. From the days of the Reformation we can trace the new interest in prophecy, especially concerning the program of God for the literal Nation of Israel.

Naturally this recognition of Israel as God's indestructible nation led to a new concept of what the true Church really is. It is given in the parable of the pearl. It was one pearl taken from the side of Him who died that we might live. The true Church consists of individuals who have by personal faith in Jesus Christ become members of His Body. Mere membership in the church organization, entered by birth or baptism or ordinance or confirmation, does not make one a Christian. It must be a vital experience of the new birth by personal faith in Christ. The Lord is calling out from all nations, peoples, tongues, denominations, a people for His Name, the true Church. The Church cannot and does not save — it is Christ alone who can bear the name SAVIOUR!

Today the first six historic periods of Church history are almost completed. We are now in that period of the hidden treasure and the precious pearl. Within the past few decades more prophecies concerning Israel, God's treasure, have been fulfilled than during the past nineteen hundred years. The unprecedented activity in Israel, the prominent place the nation has assumed in the world, the return to the land of Israel,

have pointed up the nearness of our Lord's return and the redemption of the hidden treasure.

At the same time the pearl is about to be taken by the
Divine Seeker, the Lord Jesus. While all around are movements
of compromise and mechanical union of various religious groups,
the Lord is separating the true believers, members of His Body,
and drawing them together in protest against the lack of separation, the compromise with error, the laxity of morals, the
apostasy of organized religion. Only one more thing lies ahead
— the return of Christ, then the judgment of the wicked and
the final redemption of the elect.

The Dragnet

This is the parable of the dragnet. It is a picture of the consummation of the age, the return of the Lord Jesus, and the
judgment of the tares. The great day of separation is at hand.
Then those who have paraded under false colors and were only
identified with Christendom instead of Christ, members of a
church but strangers to the One True Church, will be shown
up as the pretenders they are. How important, therefore, to
make sure that we have salvation and not mere religion. The
Bible admonishes us to:

> Examine yourselves, whether ye be in the faith; prove your
> own selves. Know ye not your own selves, how that Jesus
> Christ is in you, except ye be reprobates? (II Corinthians
> 13:5).

Do not rest until you know beyond a doubt that you have
Bible salvation. It is a solemn thought to recognize the fact
that many will expect to be saved and yet will be cast out in
the end. The importance of this great truth is emphasized by
the Lord Jesus:

> Strive to enter in at the strait gate: for many, I say unto
> you, will seek to enter in, and shall not be able.
> When once the master of the house is risen up, and hath
> shut to the door, and ye begin to stand without, and to
> knock at the door, saying, Lord, Lord, open unto us; and
> he shall answer and say unto you, I know you not whence
> ye are:
> Then shall ye begin to say, We have eaten and drunk
> in thy presence, and thou hast taught in our streets.
> But he shall say, I tell you, I know you not whence ye
> are; depart from me, all ye workers of iniquity (Luke 13:
> 24-27).

The time of separation is at hand. The judgment is coming, and Christ is knocking at the heart's door of some of you for the very last time. Soon, all too soon, the door will be shut, and then you will do the knocking but He who knocked in vain at your heart's door will then refuse to open. But it is not yet too late. The Lord Jesus is still patiently standing outside the door waiting for you to open and let Him in. Every passing minute is a reminder that the time is running out and tomorrow may be too late.

Would you like to be *sure* that all is well with your soul? Then listen, come as a helpless sinner to the Lord, believe His promise of salvation, and rest in the Word of God. Right where you are, stop, and confess your own sinfulness, believe God's promise, that — ". . . whosoever shall call upon the name of the Lord shall be saved" (Romans 10:13).

Chapter Fifteen

THE RAGING NATIONS

Until now in our study of this mystery age between the first and Second Coming of Jesus, we have dealt with two classes of people in this dispensation, Jews and Christians, the Kingdom nation in rejection and the Church being called out. There is a third group who assume a prominent role in the prophetic program for this age; viz. the Gentile nations. The program and progress (?) of the nations and their final judgment are clearly described in many passages of the Word of God. Judgment upon them is sure, but will not be executed until He comes again.

The second Psalm, the first of the so-called Messianic Psalms, is a prophecy of this present dispensation and covers the history of the nations in advance, from the first coming of Christ to His Second Coming. It covers the same period of time as the seven parables of the Kingdom during this mystery age.

Why do the heathen [nations] rage, and the people imagine a vain thing?

The kings of the earth set themselves, and the rulers take counsel together, against the Lord, and against his anointed, saying,

Let us break their bands asunder, and cast away their cords from us.

He that sitteth in the heavens shall laugh: the Lord shall have them in derision.

Then shall he speak unto them in his wrath, and vex them in his sore displeasure.

Yet have I set my king upon my holy hill of Zion.

I will declare the decree: the Lord hath said unto me, Thou art my Son; this day have I begotten thee.

Ask of me, and I shall give thee the heathen [nations] for thine inheritance, and the uttermost parts of the earth for thy possession.

Thou shalt break them with a rod of iron; thou shalt dash them in pieces like a potter's vessel.

Be wise now therefore, O ye kings: be instructed, ye judges of the earth.

Serve the LORD with fear, and rejoice with trembling.

Kiss the Son, lest he be angry, and ye perish from the way, when his wrath is kindled but a little. Blessed are all they that put their trust in him (Psalm 2).

This Psalm covers a period of more than nineteen hundred years, from the first coming of Christ to die, up until His glorious Second Coming to reign upon this earth. The raging of the nations was already in progress when Jesus Christ was rejected by His people and nailed to the cross. Not content with killing Him, they now seek to persecute His followers. When the early disciples were being arrested and put in prison, the disciples recognized that this was in fulfillment of this second Psalm, for we read in Acts 4 that they (the persecuted disciples) said:

Who by the mouth of thy servant David hast said, Why did the heathen rage, and the people imagine vain things?

The kings of the earth stood up, and the rulers were gathered together against the Lord, and against his Christ.

For of a truth against thy holy child Jesus, whom thou hast anointed, both Herod, and Pontius Pilate, with the Gentiles, and the people of Israel, were gathered together.

For to do whatsoever thy hand and thy counsel determined before to be done.

And now, Lord, behold their threatenings: and grant unto thy servants, that with all boldness they may speak thy word (Acts 4:25-29).

From this quotation we know that the raging of the nations against Christ goes back to Jesus' first coming and will continue till He comes again. The early Christians were not popular with the world, and it is a sad commentary on the lukewarm and insipid testimony of Christendom today in this land, that we are so popular instead of being persecuted. There is no precedent in the Bible or history that believers who are all out for Christ, and who will not compromise with the world, should enjoy the friendship and plaudits of the world. The world is against Christ, and if we fully follow Him, we too shall find out that we are not wanted. The nations rage, says David, because they are against Christ, God's anointed One. The popularity which Christians enjoy today is not an indication of the power of the Gospel but a sign of decay and conformity with a Christ-rejecting world.

ALL FORETOLD BEFORE

This is all foreshadowed in this second Psalm. The animosity of the world against the Christ of the Bible which manifested itself early in the life of the Church as we saw in Acts, chapter 4, will be restrained for a time, only to break out in all its fury just before the return of Christ. We believe that time has come. The world is today as never before rejecting the Christ of God, and accepting a pseudo-Christ, a false Christ, an imitation Christ, tolerating Him only as the founder of a great religion, while rejecting His deity, atoning death, and resurrection, and especially His personal literal coming again. A sickly, exsanguinated, compromising, ecumenical "gospel" has manufactured a clever counterfeit Christ; followers of this line love to repeat the phrases of a neo-orthodoxy, and the new evangelicalism, and call it progress over the old "blood and thunder" Gospel of days past. Scores of new translations, good, bad, and indifferent, are rolling from our presses, each one adding their little bit to the business of confusing the minds of people and producing disrespect for the Word of God. With all the translations, versions, editions, and opinions of men, people are asking, "How can we know what and who is right?" This, beloved, we firmly believe is a part of the strategy of the enemy to bring to a climax the words of David: "Why do the heathen [nations] rage, and the people imagine a vain thing?" (Psalm 2:1).

The reason, we repeat, is that the nations will not acknowledge God as the only source of help in their calamity. But all this has been foretold in minutest detail. The present wars and turmoil with starvation, famine, and revolution, the earthquakes, storms, signs in the heavens, false prophets and Christs, the apostasy of the Church and the threatened breakup of civilization, have all been foretold as signs of our Lord's return and the end of the age. No wonder the nations are in perplexity. And now add to this the threat of atomic destruction, the knowledge that the enemy possesses the know-how and the wherewithal virtually to annihilate civilization, and the words of Jesus begin to take on new meaning: ". . . and upon the earth distress of nations, with perplexity . . ." (Luke 21:25).

Let us remember that all this, man has brought upon himself. It is the result of man's inventions and astounding progress in the field of technological science. The atomic bomb is a child of man's fantastic increase of scientific knowledge. It is a staggering paradox, that man's progress (?) in the field of education and knowledge should result in the discovery of such an instrument of destruction with the potentialities of wiping out the entire civilization of this world. But all this too was foretold by the Bible.

KNOWLEDGE AND TRAVEL

In Daniel 12:4 we read: "But thou, O Daniel, shut up the words, and seal the book, even to the time of the end: many shall run to and fro, and knowledge shall be increased."

The meaning of Daniel's words could not be understood until they actually came to pass, and that would be at the time of the end. Up until this present generation we could not understand what Daniel meant by the words, "many shall run to and fro, and knowledge shall be increased." They were sealed until the *time of the end.* Today we know what Daniel meant — there is no doubt about it any more; and so we know it is the time of the end. What an accurate description of *today* we have in the phrase, "many shall run to and fro, and knowledge shall be increased."

THE AGE OF SPEED

This indeed is the age of speed and travel. Almost unbelievable is the progress in the field of rapid travel within the past few decades. In one single generation within the memory of many of us, we have come from the horse-and-buggy age into a supersonic age with jets and missiles, satellites and space ships, attaining speeds of thousands of miles per hour. In the past fifty years there has been greater progress in the field of speed and travel than man had seen in five thousand years before this century opened. It is only thirty-five years ago that Charles Lindbergh startled the slow-moving world with his non-stop flight from New York to Paris on May 21, 1927. In a third of a century Lindbergh's plane is as obsolete as a sickle or a team of oxen; his speed a mere snail's pace compared to our ultra-modern vehicles of transportation. And this is only in the field of air transportation. Equally great, if not as dramatic, has been the increase in the improvement of the automobile, fast steamships, and atomic vessels. Air travel has revolutionized society so that today millions travel all over the world and think nothing of making trips in a few hours which would have been unthinkable a few years ago by the slow means of transportation. A generation or two ago few people ever traveled more than a few miles from home; today with the world on wheels and wings, most people travel thousands of miles each year. How significant the words, "many shall run to and fro." Millions and tens of millions of cars on the highways at all hours of the day and night! On a recent holiday weekend there were said to be 70 million cars on the American highways, and our colossal highway building program at a cost of billions of dollars is a result of the fulfillment of Daniel's prophecy, "many shall run to and fro."

AGE OF DISCOVERY

Daniel mentions as a second outstanding sign of the end of the age the increase in knowledge. He says, "Many shall run to and fro (travel), and knowledge shall be increased." Never before in the history of the world has there been such a rapid increase in knowledge in every field of human endeavor. Again we can assert that the first six decades of this twentieth century have seen more progress in the fields of science, technology, and industry, than all the thousands of previous years of recorded history. With technological advances, new inventions, automation, and finally the discovery of atomic power, every sphere of human activity has been revolutionized and necessitated a complete readjustment in every field of existence — socially, economically, industrially and even spiritually. Yes, indeed, the increase in knowledge defies description. Think of the increase in knowledge as the result of the radio and television, the modern methods of automation, in the production of books, papers, magazines, and floods of other educational and "uneducational" literature. Or think of the expression, "knowledge shall be increased," as applied to the healing arts — medicine, surgery, and psychiatry. With the discovery of vaccines, serums, antibiotics, antitoxins, and other specific remedies, certain diseases such as small pox, diphtheria, yellow fever, malaria, tuberculosis, scarlet fever, and many others, have been greatly reduced and in some cases practically eliminated. Think of the increase in knowledge in the realm of astronomy, geology, and now to cap it all, in the area of nuclear physics. The atomic bomb and its successors: the hydrogen, cobalt, and N-bomb, are all children of the twentieth century. We might mention the increase in the knowledge of space travel, orbiting satellites, and moon-shots, but the most dramatic of all the discoveries implied in Daniel's words, "knowledge shall be increased," was in the discovery of nuclear fission.

THREAT OF ANNIHILATION

The atomic bomb is in a class by itself. It holds possibilities and potentialities common to no other discovery. While much of the scientific knowledge of the last days may be classified as a blessing to mankind, in providing comforts and enjoyments, and giving hope of cure in illness, not so with the atomic bomb. While we hear much about converting atomic energy into useful industrial purposes, this is completely overshadowed and blotted out by the threat of wholesale annihilation, when used for destructive purposes. The earliest atomic bomb, a crude, primitive type compared with the present bomb, killed 150,000 men, women, and children in one explosion. Today we have great stockpiles of bombs, a thousand times more lethal, and just recently Khrushchev boasted that Russia had sufficient bombs and bombers to deliver them, to wipe the western powers out of existence and blow them into oblivion.

WHAT DOES IT MEAN?

This is the result of man's increase in knowledge. He is threatening to make his own invention the means of his own destruction. Man has increased in knowledge, but *not in wisdom.* But there is a bright ray of hope. All this was already prophesied by Daniel twenty-five hundred years ago, "many shall run to and fro, and knowledge shall be increased." And Jesus said when Daniel's prophecies would come to pass then the end would be near (Matthew 24:15), and we should look for the return of the Lord. Without this hope of our Lord's return we too would be driven to despair. It is difficult to think of the discoveries in the field of nuclear fission as progress, when promoted for military purposes.

To the question, therefore, of David in Psalm 2, "Why do the heathen [nations] rage?" we can answer, "because they do not know which way to turn in this age of violence and threat of atomic destruction." Hanging over the heads of the nations is the dire, horrible fear that at any moment, some trigger-happy despot will in his Castro-onic, Hitler-ian madness drop a missile that would set the world on fire. This is why the nations rage; they have forsaken God and now in this hour of perplexity they do not know the way out. In the next chapter we shall take up the teaching of the second Psalm in the light of today's developments. May I suggest you read, or better still, memorize this up-to-date Psalm and be informed of God's plan for the days ahead.

To the believer, however, all the present day developments are no cause for fear, for he knows that it is all according to plan. It was Jesus Himself who said: "And when these things begin to come to pass, then look up, and lift up your heads; for your redemption draweth nigh" (Luke 21:28).

Chapter Sixteen

WILL MAN CONQUER SPACE?

Just before our Lord Jesus left His disciples, He informed them that although He was leaving them, He was also coming back again. Naturally the disciples were anxious to know more about this encouraging event and especially the *time* of His coming again. They asked Him, "Tell us, . . . what shall be the sign of thy coming, and of the end of the world [age]?" (Matthew 24:3). What sign will there be when these things shall come to pass? To this question Jesus answered that while the exact date would not be given, nevertheless certain signs would indicate the *nearness* of the event. Among these was one outstanding, prominent sign: wars and commotions among the nations. He said: "But when ye shall hear of wars and commotions, be not terrified: for these things must first come to pass; but the end is not [come yet] by and by" (Luke 21:9).

And in verse 25 He says:

> And there shall be signs in the sun, and in the moon, and in the stars; and upon the earth *distress of nations*, with perplexity; the sea and the waves roaring;
> Men's hearts failing them for fear, and for looking after those things which are coming on the earth: for the powers of heaven shall be shaken (Luke 21:25, 26).

Among the many unmistakable signs which would herald His soon return, our Lord lays especial stress upon international relationships. Because of a shrunken world in this technological age of speed and increase of knowledge, the fear of attack is greatly intensified. As a result the nations will grope frantically for a solution. In the constant fear of atomic attack the nations will seek a solution to the awful dilemma of technological progress, or total annihilation. Jesus describes it as "wars and commotions and distress of nations with perplexity." How descriptive of the world today! DISTRESS OF NATIONS, WITH PERPLEXITY. In these graphic, unmistakable terms Jesus spake of the "last days," the "end of the age," and gave it as one of

105

the signs of His imminent return — "distress of nations, with perplexity." Though spoken nineteen hundred years ago, no more accurate description of conditions in the world right this minute could possibly be given — Distress of Nations, or Nations in Distress with perplexity! The word "distress" in the original is *sunoche* and means literally "to be pressed on all sides." The word "perplexity" in the original is *aporia* and means, "no way out." We may therefore paraphrase the passage, "and on earth the nations pressed (threatened) on all sides, with no way out." Can you imagine a better description of the conditions in the world today? The pressures are from all sides. One crisis after another is driving diplomats and statesmen into a frenzy of perplexity. Now it is the crisis in the Congo, then the Middle East, then Laos, Cuba, South America. Suddenly it shifts to Korea, now the Berlin crisis and back to Israel and the Arabs — constant pressures, compressed from every angle. Conferences, discussions, meetings of heads of state, ambassadors racing from capital to capital, while the cold war gets hotter and hotter. Nations in distress, with perplexity — pressed on every side with no seeming way out. This was Jesus' own description of the days in which we live today.

THE NEUTRON BOMB

In addition to all these disturbing and perplexing problems there is the constant threat of nuclear war, with its unspeakable implications. First it was the uranium bomb, then the hydrogen bomb; next the cobalt bomb and now the scientists are working on what may well be the ultimate in destructive powers — the neutron bomb, called for short the "N-bomb." Triggered by a fission detonator producing one million degrees of heat centigrade, it will be technology's deadliest weapon. It would kill all organic life within the range of its power, but without destroying buildings or industrial and military installations. Its power, being manifested in radiation rather than shock, would be able to wipe out an entire population without disturbing the physical structure of the area. Thus the attacker would take over an undamaged city or country with all its inhabitants dead, while the industrial and scientific equipment would be undamaged and ready to be used by the victor. What a ghastly prospect! Truly it is the answer to David's question in Psalm 2, "Why do the nations rage, and the people imagine a vain thing?" The answer lies in Jesus' words, the nations are in distress with no way to turn. They have no place to hide, for there is no apparent defense against the N-bomb. One top scientist says in essence, "We are in mortal peril, for the N-bomb would act as a death ray, doing little or no physical damage to buildings and installations, and result in no contamination, but would immediately destroy all organic life within the target area." The currently recommended shelters would be of no use whatsoever, as the N-bomb penetration would be almost unbelievable.

In this kind of a world we are living today! With all our increase in knowledge we have developed a suicidal civilization. Are we then doomed to destruction? Is there then really no place to hide? Must we live constantly under the threat of war and imminent annihilation? Man has no positive answer. He is hopeful and engages in wishful thinking, but there is only one answer and only one place to find the answer. It is in the same Book which has already infallibly predicted all these things. The unmistakable accuracy of the prophecies of the days in which we live stamps the Bible with the seal of its dependability, and so we turn to it for the solution of the problem. We call your attention again, therefore, to God's answer as found in Psalm 2, where David asks the vital question. "Why do the [nations] rage [why are they in distress], and the people imagine a vain thing [are in perplexity]?"

Then follows the reason for their distress and perplexity. Listen to it: "The kings of the earth set themselves, and the rulers take counsel together, against the LORD, and against his anointed . . ." (Psalm 2:2).

Here is God's answer to the question, *why?* Why do the nations rage? Why are the nations in distress? Why the fear and perplexity? They have rejected and ignored God in all their planning. God is not recognized in all the counsels of the nations. Man still imagines that he can solve the problem of war and destruction. One great sector of the world has openly announced its atheism, and determination to banish religion from the earth; the rest of the nations, while still professing faith in God, have not followed His Word, but by ignoring Him and rejecting His Son are as guilty as the others.

THE SIN OF THE NATIONS

David reveals in the next verse the evil intentions of the nations. Hear them saying: "Let us break their bands asunder, and cast away their cords from us" (Psalm 2:3).

Man is determined to break the limitations and restraints of God as earth dwellers, and now he aspires to go "off limits" and conquer the universe. Man's desire to conquer space is a repetition of a former abortive attempt by Satan and is in open defiance of God's plan for man on this earth. Probably never until this generation of interplanetary dreaming have we been able really to understand the words of Psalm 2:3, "Let us break their bands asunder, and cast away their cords from us."

May we suggest that in these prophetic words we have a reference to man's attempt to break through the barriers of space set by the Almighty, and which bind man to this earth. The Bible says: "The heaven, even the heavens, are the Lord's: but the earth hath he given to the children of men" (Psalm 115:16).

In Acts 17:26 we are told that God hath determined the "bounds of man's habitation," limiting him to this earth, and any attempt to break through the God-appointed barrier of space is in direct defiance of God and is in fulfillment of David's account of the proud boast of man: "Let us break his bands asunder, and cast away their cords from us" (Psalm 2:3).

MAN'S DREAM TODAY

So man in his depraved condition and darkened understanding dreams of sending a man to the moon in less than five years and from there to the very limits of the heavens. However, there is not a single verse in the Scripture to support the empty imaginations of man. As Lucifer's attempt came to naught, and man's effort to build a tower of Babel whose top would reach into Heaven was frustrated by God, so, too, man's ambitious program to "break God's bands asunder and cast their cords" from them must come to naught. The astronomical sums of money spent in this mad, futile, fruitless race for domination of the heavens is the cause of God's laughing at man's feeble efforts. In our booklet, *Next Stop the Moon*, we proved beyond a shadow of doubt that the Bible predicts the utter failure of man's plans to conquer the heavens.

What a tragedy it would be indeed if earthbound man should reach these other planets. If there are inhabitants on these planets, what would we have to offer them? What a calamity it would be if we could bring our crumbling civilization with its crime, violence, destruction, war, and bloodshed to another world. How much better if we would concentrate upon cleaning up the mess we are in before attempting to dump the mess on other worlds. Suppose we could reach another inhabited planet — what could we offer them? Would we want to impose on another world the kind of a civilization we have here with its war, crime, evil, death, and constant fear of annihilation by an atomic war? Better we should remain here, and instead of wasting billions in a futile effort to export our mess to others, and bankrupting the nations, we should stay at home and clean up our own backyard.

THE WISDOM OF MAN

All this goes by the name of progress. After millenniums of a progressive (so-called) civilization, the world is in the worst situation of all time. It is one crisis after another, with the wealth of the nations wasted in a vain effort to bring peace without the Prince of Peace. With millions starving in the world, and the underprivileged nations in rebellion, with national debt mounting to precarious heights, we are spending our time and wealth in a fruitless, hopeless fiasco. Truly the description of nations in commotion as described in Psalm 2 fits this present generation in every detail: "Why do the heathen [nations] rage, and the people imagine a vain [hopeless] thing?"

As believers in the Bible, we are therefore mostly interested in what God thinks about all this. Our Scripture says that God laughs at all these schemes of men. To God it is all foolishness, for the wisdom of man is foolishness with God. In our coming chapter we shall see why God laughs at man's vain endeavors. But He will not keep silence forever, but one of these days He will utter His voice, step down from His Throne and, after judging the nations, set up His glorious Kingdom here upon the earth. We would therefore assert once more, the only solution to man's dilemma, the only answer to the distress of nations, the only hope for a world facing atomic annihilation is the coming of the Prince of Peace, the return of Jesus Christ according to His promise. There is no other hope, no other answer. Our hope does not lie in peace treaties by independable man, or in defeating communism or in worldwide revival, or in the conversion of the world in this generation, but in the personal return of Jesus Christ. Jesus said: "And when these things begin to come to pass, then look up, and lift up your heads; for your redemption draweth nigh" (Luke 21:28).

Nowhere in the Bible are we told to look for, wait for, or watch for anything else but the return of Christ. He is the only answer to every problem in the world.

Chapter Seventeen

WHY GOD LAUGHS

Why do the heathen [nations] rage, and the people imagine a vain thing? (Psalm 2:1).

This is the question David voiced under inspiration, as he looked into the future to the end of the age. That David was speaking of the last days, the very days in which we are living, is evident from the verses which follow in the light of present day developments. It may well be a prophecy of the present race among the nations to conquer space and invade the heavenly bodies. After asking the question, "Why do the heathen [nations] rage?" he gives both the reason and the outcome of man's attempt to conquer the heavens. He asks, *why?* Why do the nations propose an impossible feat? Why do they imagine they can colonize the moon and Mars and Venus? It is a vain dream, a fantastic delusion, supported neither by logic, science, nor the Bible. It is in defiance of the Word of God and its clear teaching that man's place is on this earth, and his designs to go beyond these bounds are doomed to failure. We can hardly mistake the words:

> The kings of the earth set themselves, and the rulers take counsel together, against the Lord, and against his anointed, saying,
> Let us break their bands asunder, and cast away their cords from us (Psalm 2:2, 3).

After telling us of the raging nations in rebellion against God's limitations upon man's habitation, the rest of the Psalm gives an orderly, chronological account of the outcome. He mentions the following things in their order. While the nations are raging and imagining vain things, God is laughing. But His silence will be broken, for after a time God speaks in His wrath and comes to judge the nations. Next He will set up the Kingdom and bring in world peace. All this is given in Psalm 2, and to bring it clearly before you, we call your at-

110

tention to the orderly progress of the Psalm and you will have an accurate outline of the course of this age up till the Second Coming of Christ and the setting up of the Messianic Kingdom of peace.

The Psalm opens with the question: "Why do the heathen rage, and the people imagine a vain thing?" (Psalm 2:1).

Then there follows a description of how the raging of the nations manifests itself:

> The kings of the earth set themselves, and the rulers take counsel together, against the LORD, and against his anointed, saying,
> Let us break their bands asunder, and cast away their cords from us (Psalm 2:2, 3).

This is a scene of conferences and top-level meetings among the heads of state, kings and rulers. They counsel together in a united effort to attain a certain goal. This suggests a united effort by the nations, for it says they "take counsel together." But it is not a council or conference or meeting to determine the will of God, nor to acquaint themselves with the Word of God. Instead, David says this counseling of the nations is *against* the Lord and *against* His anointed (Psalm 2:2). God is not in the planning of the world organizations. Jesus is never consulted or owned or recognized. The revelation of the Bible is never appealed to, but instead foolish man pursues his own program and boldly claims he can solve his problem by himself. God is not in all their thoughts.

BREAK THE BANDS

Now notice the conclusions this council of nations reaches, and the program they propose. There are the resolutions adopted concerning God and His anointed, the Messiah Jesus Christ: "Let us break their bands asunder, and cast away their cords from us" (Psalm 2:3).

The words translated "bands" and "cords" both imply restraints or limitations beyond which they cannot go. The word translated "bands" is *moserah* and is rendered "halter" in my lexicon. The word translated "cords" is *aboth* and signifies a metal rope or a chain. God has put certain restraints and limitations on man beyond which God will not permit him to go. God has put a "halter" on the activities of man to keep him from running wild. He has placed him on a chain which determines just how far he may reach. Man imagines there is no limit to what God will allow him to discover and develop on this earth, but when he reaches out into space beyond his appointed boundaries of earth, and seeks to invade the heavens, then God places a check, a halter upon him. Interestingly enough, the first syllable of halter is *halt*. One of these days God will call a "halt" to man's wild dreams at breaking the chain which binds him to the earth.

Today man chafes against the narrow confines of this little shrunken world. With the tremendous advances in the field of invention, technology, and all the science, the telescopic discoveries of billions of other worlds in space, the world has become too small to satisfy him, and so he looks beyond this earth and vainly imagines he can defy God's restraints, and says: "Let us break their bands asunder, and cast away their cords from us" (Psalm 2:3). Let us break through the divinely set barriers.

What Is God Doing?

Now man has had his say, he has made his boast; let us see what God thinks of it all. Notice a startling verse which tells us God's reaction and response to man's puny plans: "He that sitteth in the heavens shall laugh: the Lord shall have them in derision" (Psalm 2:4).

God sees and observes all that is going on. He is not, however, just a disinterested observer. Yet He seemingly does not interfere with man's vain schemes and dreams. How frequently we hear the question, "If there is a God in Heaven, why doesn't He interfere and put an end to the bungling of the nations? If God is sovereign, why does He allow all the violence and suffering and despoliation? Why does He permit wars, the bombing of whole cities, hospitals, and children's homes, laying waste whole countries and spilling the blood of countless thousands of innocent victims who had neither part nor voice in bringing it about? Why, oh why does God keep silent? Why doesn't He stop all this?" We believe the Bible gives the answer.

God is going to let man himself prove the utter depravity of human nature, the incorrigible wickedness of the human heart, the absolute failure of man's efforts to govern himself, the utter uselessness of all man's efforts and highest achievements to abolish war, crime and disease, and the impossibility of bringing in an age of peace and prosperity by man's efforts. Man must be brought to the end of himself; he must be convinced of his hopelessness without God. God today is proving man's failure with a vengeance. After centuries and millenniums of our flaunted civilization, and boasting of human progress, with its advance in education and reform, scientific evolution, the heart of man has not been improved one bit. The unregenerate heart of man is not changed by all these developments. In fact, the potentialities and possibilities of wickedness in the natural man are increased and augmented by culture and education, instead of being improved. The more educated a sinner is, the more dangerous he becomes. An educated criminal is far more to be feared than an ignorant one. A smart burglar is more to be feared than a dumb one.

The same is true of the nations with all their progress, culture, education, technological advances, and scientific progress. With all this added knowledge, the world has never seen conditions more ominous than today. Living in the shadow of atomic destruction, the world is gripped by fear, and Jesus' words come with tremendous impact: "Men's hearts failing them for fear, and for looking after those things which are coming on the earth: for the powers of heaven shall be shaken" (Luke 21:26).

No wonder God is said to laugh at it all, for God's program calls for all these things to continue, till God steps in. Nowhere in the entire Bible is there a single verse to support the contention that this world will become better and better until at last by the efforts of man in the field of education, science, and the preaching of a watered-down, social "gospel," man will finally learn his lesson and the age will climax in a great worldwide revival, and then wars will be abolished, and the nations live in peace. *No! No!* My friend, the Bible knows nothing of such a program! Instead the Bible teaches without exception that the world will grow worse and worse. It warns us that in the last days perilous times shall come and this age will climax in the most terrible war of all history. The Bible teaches that there is going to be another World War indescribably more devastating than all the wars of history combined, and except for the intervention of God in this atomic conflict "no flesh shall be saved." In speaking of the closing days of this dispensation, Jesus says: "And except those days should be shortened, there should no flesh be saved" (Matthew 24:22).

This we can now easily understand in this atomic age when Russia already boasts she has sufficient nuclear weapons ready for immediate use to wipe the Western Allies from the face of the earth. All man's efforts to bring an end to the mounting international problems which cause the "distress of nations, with perplexity," are doomed to failure. The only hope is the intervention of God by the return of the Lord Jesus Christ.

David says: "He that sitteth in the heavens shall laugh: the Lord shall have them in derision" (Psalm 2:4).

The word rendered "derision" means "to mock or laugh to scorn." Not often is it said that God laughs, and in every case it is laughter at man's final attempts to save himself. Concerning wicked men, David says: "The Lord shall laugh at him: for he seeth that his day is coming" (Psalm 37:13).

Concerning the godless nations of the end time we read: "But thou, O Lord, shalt laugh at them; thou shalt have all the heathen [nations] in derision" (Psalm 59:8).

Once again we read about the laughter of God, "Because I have called, and ye refused. . . . and would none of my reproof: I also will laugh at your calamity; I will mock when your fear cometh" (Proverbs 1:24-26).

Yes, God is said to laugh at man's vain efforts to make himself God. God laughs at the nations as they strive for peace, while rejecting the Prince of Peace. God laughs at man's attempts to create a one-world of united peoples without the coming of the only King and Potentate who alone can set up God's united Kingdom. God laughs at man as he seeks to unite all religions into one great world church by substituting man as the head instead of Jesus Christ as the Head and Cornerstone. God laughs at man's vain dream of invading the heavens and conquering space. He laughs at man's puny efforts to solve his own vexing problems. He looks upon the nations in commotion, He hears their saber rattling, He notes their boastful plans and display of physical power. He, before whom the nations are as "a drop of a bucket, and are counted as the small dust of the balance" (Isaiah 40:15), laughs at man's strutting and threatening.

However, He will not always remain silent, for after David says that God laughs at their folly, he continues: "Then shall he speak unto them in his wrath, and vex them in his sore displeasure" (Psalm 2:5).

This is to be the end of man's bungling, for now God finally speaks. In verse 3 man speaks: "Let us break their bands asunder, and cast away their cords from us" (Psalm 2:3).

Now it is God's turn to speak, and as He does, the judgment falls upon the nations. First God will speak from the air to call home His Church, and the time of tribulation and judgment will be ushered in. This is briefly described in verse 5. The Lord will "speak unto them in his wrath, and vex them in his sore displeasure" (Psalm 2:5).

At the voice of God two things will happen. First the Church will be raptured — caught up out of the earth before judgment falls. This Paul describes in the well-known passage in I Thessalonians 4: "For the Lord himself shall descend from heaven with a shout . . ." (I Thessalonians 4:16).

The dead in Christ will be raised, and all living believers raptured. But this same shout which calls home the Church will be the shout of judgment for those who remain. God will speak in His wrath and for seven awful years judgment will be let loose upon a Christ-rejecting world. And at the end God will speak once more. What God will say then to the nations we shall take up in the next chapter.

When the Lord comes every believer will be gone, and the antichrist, the false king, will take over, only to be defeated by our Lord Jesus the King, when He comes for His own. And so the most pressing question is, Are you ready for the most certain event in the future — the coming of the Lord?

Chapter Eighteen

WHEN GOD SPEAKS

For nineteen hundred years there has been no voice, no message from Heaven. With the close of the book of Revelation, Heaven has been silent except for the sound of laughter. All claims of additional messages or revelations from Heaven, after the close of the book of the Revelation, are a deception and a fraud. For nineteen hundred years the nations have been raging and imagining vain things and apparently there has been no direct interference by God. But God laughs at man's puny efforts to bring in a kingdom of peace, a united world by the efforts of men. God laughs at all of it. In reply to the threat of the heathen nations, "Let us break their bands asunder, and cast away their cords from us" (Psalm 2:3), the Psalmist says, "He that sitteth in the heavens shall laugh" (Psalm 2:4). We sincerely believe that the expression, "Let us break their bands asunder, and cast away their cords from us," has reference, among other things, to man's present dream of conquering the heavens by space travel and breaking through the barriers set by the Creator. Once before men made an attempt to conquer space, when they builded a tower "whose top may reach unto heaven" (Genesis 11:4). Today's fantastic dream of interplanetary travel bears a striking resemblance to the crude effort made at the tower of Babel. Notice the similarity of the description. At the tower of Babel they "said one to another"; that is, they took counsel together. And what did they say? "*Let us* make us a name" (Genesis 11:3, 4). The same words are used in Psalm 2 – "*Let us* break their bands asunder, and cast away their cords from us" (Psalm 2:3). Again man speaks in defiance of God.

THE STRIKING PARALLEL

There is a striking parallel between the building of Babel and man's plans for today. The tower was, among other things:

1. A godless program; for it was all man's efforts, and God

116

was not once recognized. They said, "Let us."

2. It was an attempt to maintain a united world and to oppose segregation and promote integration. This is evident from the purpose expressed in Genesis 11:4, "lest we be scattered abroad upon the face of the whole earth"; that is, lest we be segregated. It was fear of disintegration which prompted the building of the tower.

3. Its goal was Heaven. The top of the tower was to reach Heaven. It was indeed an ambitious space program.

4. It was to make themselves a name. Man wanted to maintain his leadership. Today the mad race in space exploration seems again to be motivated by the desire to keep ahead of the other nations. What advantage would there be in reaching the moon first, except for prestige and "making a name"? One cannot conceive of any other practical value of any excuse for wasting countless billions just to keep up with the Joneses.

5. But finally, notice how it ended. It came to a sudden stop by the coming down of the Lord, confusing their speech and frustrating all their plans. Once again the Lord will come to bring man's plans to naught.

THE SPEAKING LORD

This David tells us in Psalm 2. After a period of patient silence while God laughs, the time finally comes for God to step in, and so we read: "Then shall he speak unto them in his wrath, and vex them in his sore displeasure" (Psalm 2:5).

The next event, therefore, we believe, will be the shout from the air, the return of Jesus to take *out* His Church, to be followed by a period of unprecedented tribulation and sorrow as expressed in the phrase, "and vex them in his sore displeasure." This period of time is called the Day of the Lord, the Time of Jacob's Trouble, and the Tribulation. At the close the Lord will return to the earth with His Bride, and set up His Millennial Kingdom, after Satan is cast into the bottomless pit. This is when God speaks in judgment to the nations. Joel tells us: "The LORD also shall roar out of Zion, and utter his voice from Jerusalem . . ." (Joel 3:16).

And what does God say to the nations? "Yet have I set my king upon my holy hill of Zion" (Psalm 2:6).

Notice carefully the first word in this verse. It is the word *yet* — "*Yet* have I set my king upon my holy hill of Zion." In spite of all the raging of godless nations, in spite of man's frantic efforts to solve the problems of this world, in spite of the bid of the antichrist to dethrone the Lord Jesus and usurp His dominion, *yet, in spite of all this,* "I have set my king upon my holy hill of Zion." My plan and My program is going through in spite of man. The same Jesus, who nineteen hundred years ago was rejected and crucified, is coming back to bring in the age of peace and tranquillity for which the nations are hopelessly striving today. And that Kingdom will not be on the moon or Mars, but right here upon this earth. His throne will be in Jerusalem, and He will demonstrate His power and authority in the very place where He was rejected before. This King will reign in God's holy hill of Zion — in Jerusalem.

THE SON SPEAKS

That this King is Jesus is made clear in the next verse. In verse 3 the rulers of the earth speak, "Let us cast the restraints of the Almighty from us." Then the Spirit speaks through David, "He that sitteth in the heavens shall laugh: the Lord shall have them in derision." And then the Father speaks in His wrath and says: "Yet have I set my king upon my holy hill of Zion" (Psalm 2:6).

And then the Son responds in these prophetic words in the next verse:

I will declare the decree: the LORD hath said unto me, Thou art my Son; this day have I begotten thee.
Ask of me, and I shall give thee the heathen [nations] for thine inheritance, and the uttermost parts of the earth for thy possession (Psalm 2:7, 8).

And then in verse 9 we have the character of His reign in righteousness and justice: "Thou shalt break them with a rod of iron; thou shalt dash them in pieces like a potter's vessel" (Psalm 2:9).

This then is the program of God as given in the second Psalm. It is a program extending from the first coming of Christ when He was rejected, to the setting up of the Kingdom at the consummation of the ages. That this period of Gentile raging goes way back to Christ's first coming is seen from the fact that the early Church when persecuted quoted this same Psalm as applying already to the rulers, Herod and Pontius Pilate (Acts 4:25-27).

For almost two millenniums now the nations have pursued

their futile efforts to bring in an age of peace and universal prosperity, only to find conditions growing worse and worse, while God laughs at man's fruitless, futile, desperate attempts to prevent his own destruction. Soon the Lord will shout from Heaven, rain judgment upon the nations as He vexes them in His sore displeasure, and then, when God has demonstrated the utter incorrigibility of the wicked human heart, He will set up His Kingdom at the Second Coming of Christ, and bring in the golden age of man's dreams, but according to the plan of God. And so we have in this Psalm a chronological account of the course of this age and how it will end.

THE NEXT EVENT

These are terrible days in which we live and yet they are wonderful days. For while wickedness and violence are increasing on every hand, the Bible tells us that "all these things *must* come to pass." All that we see around about us is in fulfillment of the sure word of prophecy. Not a single thing is happening except according to the program of God. Every single detail of the present world conditions was foreknown by God and foretold by the prophets and by our Lord Jesus Christ. While the unbeliever knows not what to think of conditions in the world today, the regenerated student of the Word sees in all these things the fulfillment of His Word and the evidences of the faithfulness of God.

The next event in the program of God is the coming of the Lord Jesus Christ from Heaven. I am bringing these messages in the firm conviction that we are rapidly approaching the end of an age — an age that will close with the sudden translation of the blood-bought Church of the Lord Jesus Christ. God have mercy on the Christian who does not study the Word and is ignorant of the signs of the times. The Lord has said so clearly, "When these things begin to come to pass, then look up . . . for your redemption draweth nigh" (Luke 21:28).

What a blessed thing to have this Bible, and we who believe it are not left in the dark. No wonder that those who do not believe the Book are groping in fear and trembling. For such Jesus predicted this "distress of nations, with perplexity." And David calls it the raging of the nations, and imagining a vain thing. Our only hope is from above. Truly there is no place left to hide on this earth. We have been told by those who should know, that there is no shelter which can protect us from the bombs being perfected today. The only way *out* is *up*. It is the only way of safety, the only source of hope. Soon the Lord will open the heavens to receive His own, before that great and terrible Day of the Lord breaks upon an unbelieving, Christ-rejecting, suicidal world. The most important question, therefore, is: "Do you know Christ, and are you among those who will be saved when judgment falls, and who according to Jesus in Luke 21 shall 'escape all these things that shall come to pass, and to stand before the Son of man' (Luke 21:36)?"

THE LAST INVITATION

We find that this prophetic Psalm ends with a warning and an invitation. Notice the solemn warning to the nations: "Be wise now therefore, O ye kings: be instructed, ye judges of the earth. Serve the LORD with fear, and rejoice with trembling" (Psalm 2:10, 11).

And then follows a gracious, personal invitation. The nations rage and prate about conquering space while living in the shadow of destruction, and although God laughs at man's feeble efforts, He is still extending His gracious call to come out from among the ungodly crowd and be saved. And so the Psalm ends with an invitation and a benediction: "Kiss the Son, lest he be angry, and ye perish from the way, when his wrath is kindled but a little. Blessed are all they that put their trust in him" (Psalm 2:12).

The word translated "kiss" comes from a root meaning "to become attached." A kiss is a symbol of attachment. Someone has translated the word as "to lick the hand." As a dog comes to its master and affectionately licks his hand, so we are to show our attachment to the Son. Licking the hand is a symbol of obedience, love, devotion, attachment and faithfulness. The invitation, "Kiss the Son," means "attach yourself" to Christ. Ally yourself with Him and be safe. Of all who thus receive the Son, God says: "Blessed [happy] are all they that put their trust in him" (Psalm 2:12).

Chapter Nineteen

THE ONE TRUE CHURCH

Man is by nature an incurably inquisitive being. He not only is concerned about his presence here on earth, but wants to know where he came from. He would also like to lift the curtain to reveal what lies ahead and so he resorts to everything except the Bible — to witchcraft, astrology, necromancy and countless superstitions to satisfy his hunger for the occult and unknown. He is not satisfied to dwell on earth alone, but dreams of interplanetary travel and is already planning residence on the moon and Mars and other planets. All of this is in the realm of speculation and guesswork. How refreshing, therefore, to be able to turn to a source of information which has never failed. The outline of future events as gathered from the Scriptures may be stated in eight chronological steps culminating in the New Heaven and the New Earth, and perfect peace and enjoyment forevermore. These eight events or steps are:

1. The Translation of the Church
2. The Great Tribulation
3. The Battle of Armageddon
4. The Second Coming of Christ
5. The Millennial Reign
6. The Final Rebellion of Satan
7. The Judgment of the Wicked
8. The New Heaven and the New Earth

Bear these eight steps in mind and watch world events fall into place in this great program. The next and the imminent event is the translation of the Church of Jesus Christ. To place anything, any event, before this event is to make void the admonition of Jesus to watch for His return, and to destroy its imminency. Yet in spite of the clear teaching of the Bible there are sincere and honest Bible students who teach that the Church must pass through part or all of the Tribulation. It is an important, a burning, a vital question. Some of the most frequent questions which we receive from our listeners are: "What about the Church in the Day of the Lord? Will the Church have to pass through the Tribulation, all or part of it? Will all believers be raptured, or will some of them have to remain behind?"

At this point it is necessary, to avoid misunderstanding, to define what we mean by the word "church." There is great misunderstanding as to the exact meaning of "the church" as used in Scripture. A great deal of confusion has existed in the minds of people in all ages. There are those who think of a church as a denomination or a sect. Others think of a church as a building of brick and mortar or wood. Still others think of a church as a local group to the exclusion of all others. However, the Bible teaches no such thing. There are no denominations whatsoever to be found in the Scriptures, for there is only one true Church, not limited to any group, nationality, tribe, or color. This one true Church, called also the body of Christ, is composed of all who since the day of Pentecost have received Christ as their Saviour and Lord, have believed on Him, and have been born again by the Word of God and by the Spirit of God. This Church, this body of Christ, was born on the day of Pentecost, and since then countless millions have been added by the Spirit of God, all in the same way — by being baptized in the Spirit in response to the Gospel, and grafted into the same body, the one true Church. There is then only one true Church, consisting of all born-again believers of all ages, whether Jew or Gentile, white or colored, rich or poor, high or low. All are one body in Christ. This is the one and only true Church which the Scripture recognizes.

I can immediately hear someone object and say, "Does not the Bible definitely teach that there are also many churches?" Paul, for instance, mentions the church in Corinth, and Ephesus, and Colosse, and John in the Revelation mentions seven separate churches in Asia Minor alone. The difficulty is solved when we remember that there is a difference between *the* Church and *a* church or several churches. The churches in these different localities were so called only because in them were represented some of the members of the *one true Church*. In Corinth, in Ephesus, in Thessalonica, were groups of believers, members of the body of Christ, who came together to remember the Lord, study His Word and pray. Insofar as there were believers and members of the body of Christ in these local assemblies, they represented and were part of the one true Church, and are called "a church" in a certain locality. It was the saints *in* these places who constituted "the church of such and such a place."

All these various members in the different assemblies were, however, members of the one true spiritual Church, the body of Christ. However, the custom of calling a building a church is entirely unscriptural. Buildings are never called "a church." It is the members who are the Church, and just because they meet in a certain building with a steeple, a tower, and a bell, does not necessarily make that building a church. Take the saints out of that building and put in a bar and the same building becomes a saloon. The Church then is a living body, a building of living stones, for God dwelleth not in temples made with hands. We have emphasized this because we feel that there is a danger of being so interested in embellishing and worshiping a building, its architecture, its altar, its pews, its appointments, and its program, that we miss the real meaning of what the Church of Christ really is. Two or three believers meeting in the name of the Lord Jesus Christ whether it be in a woodshed or cathedral, in a hut or in a costly, ornate building, constitute a church because they are members of the one true Church; while the most beautiful cathedral may be the very synagogue of Satan. Just a million-dollar pile of stones and mortar does not constitute a church where God dwells. Paul declares in Acts 17:24 that "God dwelleth not in temples made with hands."

Now this immediately raises a highly practical question. Do you belong only to *a* church, or do you belong to *the* one true Church? On your answer to this question depends your eternal destiny. Unless you have been born again and have become a member by faith in Jesus Christ, then you are still outside the one true Church and lost forever; you may belong to every religious organization in the world, be baptized by sprinkling, pouring, and immersion, go to church every day, repeat your prayers, memorize the dogmas and creeds of the church, live a good religious life, and yet be lost forever and end up in an eternal Hell. It was to just such a fine, upright, religious churchman, Nicodemus, that Jesus said, "Ye must be born again." God help you to ask yourself, "Do I belong to *the* Church, or do I merely belong to *a* church?" The most important question therefore is: How can I become a member of the one true Church which is the body of Christ? There is only one way — you must be born into it, and you cannot enter it by any other method. You can "join" a church, but you enter *the Church* by a divine act of the Spirit of God called the new birth. You can erect a church building by laying one dead stone upon another, but *the* Church of Jesus Christ is composed of living stones, not merely joined, but organically united, a living part of Christ, the Chief Cornerstone. This is the result of the new birth from above, and it is therefore called the general assembly and church of the *firstborn*, which are written in Heaven (Hebrews 12:23).

And so we would ask you: Are you a member of that body? Have you been born into the family of Heaven by a definite act of faith in Jesus Christ as your personal Saviour? If not, then every other earthly relationship leaves you still a lost sinner on the way to an eternal Hell. How terrible the very thought, a member of a church but still on the way to perdition.

There is then only one true Church consisting of all true believers in the Lord Jesus. Many of the members of this Church are already in Heaven. Some of us are still here upon the earth, while there are still others which have not yet been born. All of these who are upon the earth when Jesus returns will be raptured without dying.

The next word we must define is the "rapture." By the rapture we mean the sudden translation of these believers who are living when Christ comes, members of the one true Church from every nation, tribe and people, color and station, who will be immediately transferred into the clouds of Heaven with new redeemed bodies at Christ's coming. The dead saints will rise first, to be followed in the twinkling of an eye by the sudden change of all living believers, exchanging their mortal bodies for eternal, incorruptible, spiritual bodies; then these resurrected believers and the changed living saints will be caught up together to meet the Lord in the air. We dare to be absolutely dogmatic about this and state it without apology, for in the Word we read these words which are unmistakable:

For the Lord himself *shall* descend from heaven with a shout, with the voice of the archangel, and with the trump of God: and the dead in Christ *shall* rise first:

Then we which are alive and remain *shall* be caught up together with them in the clouds, to meet the Lord in the air: and so *shall* we ever be with the Lord (I Thessalonians 4:16, 17).

Four times the word *shall* is used in these two verses. This then we call the "Rapture of the Church." This passage alone standing by itself should be sufficient to establish the resurrection and the Rapture of the Church at Jesus' coming.

Before closing this particular chapter, we want to comment on a third word, the "tribulation." The Bible teaches that immediately following the Rapture, but preceding the Second Coming of the Lord Jesus to this earth to set up His Kingdom and to reign, there will be a brief and intense period of unprecedented sorrow, suffering, and tribulation. It is called by various names: the Tribulation, the Day of the Lord, the day of vengeance of our God, the time of Jacob's trouble, the day of judgment, and more specifically, the Great Tribulation. During this time of intense, indescribably terrible trouble upon the earth, the antichrist, the man of sin, will reign. Israel shall undergo her greatest persecution of all time. The nations of the world will be visited with unprecedented disasters and Hell itself will break loose upon this wicked, Christ-rejecting earth. Concerning this tribulation our Lord Jesus Christ Himself said: "For then shall be great tribulation, such as was not since the beginning of the world to this time, no, nor ever shall be" (Matthew 24:21).

This tribulation will end only at Jesus' coming, for He says again in Matthew 24,

> Immediately after the tribulation of those days *shall* the sun be darkened, and the moon *shall* not give her light, and the stars *shall* fall from heaven, and the powers of the heavens *shall* be shaken.
>
> And then *shall* appear the sign of the Son of man in heaven: and then *shall* all the tribes of the earth mourn, and they *shall* see the Son of man coming in the clouds of heaven with power and great glory (Matthew 24:29, 30).

Surely the language could hardly be plainer than these words of our Lord Jesus Christ Himself. The Bible is unmistakably clear that there is a day of great tribulation coming, followed by the public appearing of Jesus Christ to set up His Kingdom on the earth. However, the Rapture of the Church, or as it is called in Scripture, the Translation, will take place before this terrible day of the Lord is loosed upon the world. This event, the Rapture of the Church *before* the Tribulation, is called "that blessed hope" of the Church. If the Church is to go through the Tribulation as some teach, then it is neither blessed nor hopeful, but instead a fearful looking for judgment which is to come upon this world. The only thing we are told to look for is the return of Christ. One of these days, just as sure as Christ came the first time, the heavens will open once again, and our departed loved ones come forth with redeemed, deathless, painless bodies, and we, instantaneously changed, will be joined together with them, to rise and meet our blessed Lord in the air. Not a single believer will be left behind. Only unbelievers will be left upon this earth. The Holy Spirit in personal, abiding presence will be withdrawn and the entire body of Christ will be with the Lord.

No one can deny that the Bible teaches this is going to happen some day, and no one knows when. It may happen at any moment. We therefore want to press the question: Are you ready for the coming of the Lord? I am not asking if you are ready for death. There is one thing more certain than death itself, and that is the return of Christ. The Bible distinctly teaches that all men will *not* die. At Christ's coming there will be a generation of believers who will not see death, but who will be caught away and raptured without having to experience the last enemy, death. Oh, that we might be that generation! You may have listened to the last invitation which you will ever hear. No one can promise that you will ever have another opportunity of preparing for that inevitable day of judgment, which from all appearances is terribly near. Why not receive the Lord Jesus Christ today, and be able to join with all the saints of all ages in the prayer, "Even so, come, Lord Jesus" (Revelation 22:20).

Chapter Twenty

THE PRE-TRIBULATION RAPTURE

. . . Ye men of Galilee, why stand ye gazing up into heaven? this same Jesus, which is taken up from you into heaven, shall so come in like manner as ye have seen him go into heaven (Acts 1:11).

There is nothing more sure than the Second Coming of Jesus Christ. It is surer than death itself, for when He comes a generation of believers will be translated without dying (I Corinthians 15:51). All born-again believers believe in the personal return of Christ, but they are by no means agreed on the details and order of the events. One of the most debated questions today is the one we began to consider in the previous chapter. The question is "Will the Church of Jesus Christ pass through the coming Great Tribulation, or will she be raptured before that awful day of the Lord comes upon the earth?" This is one of the burning questions of the day, and many believers are at a loss what to believe. We receive hundreds upon hundreds of letters from confused listeners who have been taught to believe that something must still happen before the Lord can come to call out His Church. They are told that before the Lord will return we must have a world-wide, sweeping revival, or Russia must invade Palestine, or the world must be converted, or we must pass through all or part of the Tribulation. All of these, however, are but attempts to delay the coming of the Lord and to rob the Church of the blessed hope of the imminent return of our Lord Jesus Christ. Throughout the history of the Church it has been consistently held by theologians that the Rapture of the Church will take place before the Tribulation comes upon the earth. However, recently, as an indication of the deception of these last days, there has been a revival of the error that the Church will have to pass through part or all of this awful coming day.

This erroneous doctrine is not by any means new or modern, but was already present as early as the apostolic age. False teaching concerning the return of Christ was rife in the days of the Apostle Paul. The first two epistles which Paul wrote, First and Second Thessalonians, were written to correct two serious errors, both of them with regard to this very subject, the return of the Lord Jesus. First Thessalonians was inspired and written to correct a misunderstanding concerning the *premillennial* Rapture or the return of the Lord Jesus Christ *before* the Millennial Kingdom was to be set up. However, Second Thessalonians was written to correct an error concerning the *pre-tribulation* Rapture, and sets forth in no uncertain terms that not only will the Lord return before the Kingdom age, the Millennium, but He will also return for His Church before the Tribulation sets in upon this earth. So let me repeat, First Thessalonians teaches the truth of the *premillennial* Rapture, while Second Thessalonians establishes the truth of the *pre-tribulation* Rapture.

The importance of this truth may be gleaned from the fact that the first letter which Paul ever wrote to the Church is almost completely occupied with the truth of the Second Coming. First Thessalonians was the first inspired letter ever to come from Paul's pen. On his second missionary journey he had spent a couple of weeks in Thessalonica preaching the Gospel of the Lord Jesus, and among other things had told them that Christ was coming again, and when He would come they (the believers) would all enter with Him into the Kingdom of our Lord here upon the earth. In this hope they were very happy. When trials and tribulations came, when they suffered for their faith and testimony, they comforted themselves with the blessed assurance of Paul's preaching of the imminent return of Christ to end all of their troubles. But then a great disappointment overtook them. Some of the believers in Thessalonica fell sick and died. As they laid them away they began to doubt and wonder: Did not Paul tell us that Jesus was coming soon, and we would all share in the Kingdom with Him? Now what about these who have been taken by the way of death? When Jesus comes, we who are alive will, of course, enter with Him into the Kingdom; but these dead — will they miss out in the reign of Christ? This problem greatly disturbed them, for they were still uninstructed in these matters. As yet they did not know the truth of the first resurrection, before the Kingdom was to be set up. Paul had evidently not found time to instruct them fully during his brief stay in Thessalonica, and so they knew nothing about the first resurrection of believers at Jesus' coming.

As soon as Paul heard about their confusion and their sorrow and frustration, he immediately sought to set their hearts at rest by a wonderful, comforting new truth, a truth never before so clearly set forth. This new revelation is the heart of this epistle, First Thessalonians chapter 4, verses 13 to 19. In this passage Paul answers the question of these believers concerning their departed loved ones. In response to their question he says:

> But I would not have you to be ignorant, brethren, concerning them which are asleep, that ye sorrow not, even as others which have no hope.
> For if we believe that Jesus died and rose again, even so them also which sleep in Jesus will God bring with him (I Thessalonians 4:13, 14).

This answered their question about those who had fallen asleep in Christ before the coming of the Lord. They will come back with Him when He comes. And then Paul goes on and explains it more fully. There is no mistaking the simple language:

> For the Lord himself shall descend from heaven with a shout, with the voice of the archangel, and with the trump of God: and the dead in Christ shall rise first:
> Then we which are alive and remain shall be caught up together with them in the clouds, to meet the Lord in the air: and so shall we ever be with the Lord (I Thessalonians 4:16, 17).

In these clear and unmistakable words Paul asserts that the dead in Christ will not lose out in any of the blessings of Christ's coming, but will in fact *precede* those that are alive, for "the dead in Christ shall rise first," and not until after they have been resurrected will the living be suddenly changed to be caught away with them in the air to meet the Lord.

Comment on the passage hardly seems necessary. The language is so simple, so direct, so clear, that even a child can easily understand it, and we wonder how men can possibly mistake the words. Paul says, in essence, "Stop worrying about your loved ones who have died, as though they will miss out on something when Jesus comes." He says, "I would not have you to be ignorant concerning them which are asleep, that ye sorrow not, even as others which have no hope." Jesus is per-

sonally coming back and the first thing which will happen is
the resurrection of the believing dead who will suddenly come
up out of their graves in new, glorified, resurrection bodies;
then in a twinkling of an eye, living believers who are then
alive when Christ comes, will be instantly changed, receive
their immortal bodies, and join with the resurrected ones and
rise to meet the Lord in the air. We make no apology for repeating the simple revelation. It must be proclaimed over and
over again. We can well realize, therefore, the force of the
closing words of this passage, "Wherefore comfort one another
with these words" (I Thessalonians 4:18). In view of the fact
that this event is now nineteen hundred years nearer than when
Paul wrote these words, it should stir our hearts as never before, in the anticipation that we may indeed be that generation which shall not see death, but shall be caught up at the
shout of the Lord from the air. And what a comfort it is to
those of you who at this very moment may be mourning over
loved ones who have gone on before, and your mind has been
filled with questions. How comforting to know that when the
Lord comes these loved ones shall even precede us, and we
shall meet them, and then caught up together, rise to meet
our Lord in the air. Surely the words of Paul should be of
real strength in your faith, "Wherefore comfort one another
with these words."

Paul having settled their question, soon is faced with another
problem. Shortly after he had put these believers at rest concerning the pre-millennial Rapture, another error crept in.
Someone, we do not know who, wrote a letter, a forged letter,
claiming it was inspired by the Spirit, and signed with Paul's
name. This forged epistle was sent to the church at Thessalonica, in which this false teacher, this impostor and forger,
told these Thessalonian Christians that the tribulations they
were then experiencing were already the Tribulation. The awful sufferings and vicious persecutions they were enduring for
Christ's sake, this letter stated, were part of *the* Tribulation.
Now we can understand the tremendous disturbance which
must have resulted, for they had understood from Paul's letter
that they would escape the Tribulation, that the dead in Christ
would be raised first, and that all of them would be raptured
before the Day of the Lord would come. And now here comes
a letter with Paul's name attached, saying that they were now in
the Tribulation. This could mean only one thing — the Rap-

ture had taken place and they had been left behind. One can understand the consternation which must have reigned in the hearts of these believers. Just suppose that you awakened tomorrow morning to find that Christ had come during the night to take the Church into Heaven, and you were left behind. How would you feel? Well, that is how they must have felt in Thessalonica, and when Paul hears about it he immediately writes his second epistle to them, to correct this mistake and misconception. He wrote:

> Now we beseech you, brethren, by the coming of our Lord Jesus Christ, and by our gathering together unto him,
> That ye be not soon shaken in mind, or be troubled, neither by spirit, nor by word, nor by letter as from us, as that the day of Christ is at hand.
> Let no man deceive you by any means . . . (II Thessalonians 2:1-3).

Paul asserts that the letter which they had received was *not* from him, and it was a forgery, and he says to them, "Don't be upset by this false epistle. Whoever told you that this was the Tribulation is a deceiver."

The correct rendering of verse 2 should be, "That ye be not so soon shaken in mind or be troubled, neither by some spirit, nor by a word, nor by a letter supposedly by me, as that the day of the Lord *were already here.*" Don't you believe it, says the Apostle Paul. I never wrote that letter and its contents are false. And then follows the argument, which should settle once and for all the question, "Will the Church pass through the Tribulation?"

The expression "the day of Christ is at hand" is therefore a mistranslation and should read, "the day of the Lord has already come" or "is already present." And then Paul adds, "that day — the day of the Lord — shall not come except there first come a falling away"; and secondly, "that man of sin be revealed, the son of perdition."

Before we close this chapter we merely call attention to Paul's overwhelming argument for the pre-tribulation Rapture, and then trust you will study the matter carefully for yourselves. It is found in II Thessalonians, chapter 2, the first twelve verses. Read it carefully and prayerfully and see how Paul settles beyond all shadow of doubt the fact that the Church will *not* have to pass through any part of the Tribulation, but that we may confidently expect this event (the Rapture) to happen at any moment.

It is a serious thing, therefore, to attempt to place the Church in the Tribulation period, or to teach that anything must still happen before the Lord can come to catch away the Church. The Bible contains solemn warnings against daring to place anything before the possibility of the Lord's return. To say, therefore, that Jesus will not come for His Church until *after* the Tribulation destroys all the incentive and power of the truth of His imminent return. I personally would not dare to put anything between today and the imminent Rapture of the Church, thereby becoming guilty of the sin of delaying His coming. Anything which destroys the imminency, the possibility of His any-moment return, robs us of that blessed hope, for the greatest incentive to holiness and evangelism and soul-winning and service throughout the history of the Church has always been the blessed promise of His Word, "Because thou hast kept the word of my patience, I also will keep thee from the hour of temptation, which shall come upon all the world, to try them that dwell upon the earth" (Revelation 3:10). And only thus can the words of our Lord mean anything at all when He says, "Watch, therefore, for ye know not what hour your Lord doth come."

Chapter Twenty-one

THAT BLESSED HOPE

The first clear revelation concerning the Rapture of the Church is given in First Thessalonians, chapter 4. This new revelation made the Christians in Thessalonica happy and comforted them in their affliction. Paul had assured the Christians in Thessalonica the Lord was coming back to take out the Church — then set up His glorious millennial reign.

But then some practical joker, a sadistic deceiver, had written a letter to the church, telling them that they were even then passing through the tribulation. The sorrows and troubles they were experiencing for the testimony of Christ, they were told, were already the tribulation upon earth. Now since they had understood Paul to say that the Rapture would precede the Tribulation, this news would mean that they had been left behind, and naturally they were greatly disturbed. Great fear and confusion was the result. The Apostle Paul hears about it and writes this second epistle to the Thessalonians for the express purpose of immediately correcting this tragic misunderstanding. Please notice carefully Paul's answer:

Now we beseech you, brethren, by the coming of our Lord Jesus Christ, and by our gathering together unto him,

That ye be not soon shaken in mind, or be troubled, neither by spirit, nor by word, nor by letter as [though it came] from us, as that the day of Christ is at hand (II Thessalonians 2:1,2).

Literally, "as though the Day of the Lord — the Tribulation — were now here." Paul immediately denies having had anything to do with the writing of this spurious letter, and then issues a very solemn warning. He says: "Let no man deceive you by any means . . ." (II Thessalonians 2:3).

We would repeat that warning — let no man deceive you by any means! Then there follows the most glorious revelation of the Lord in answer to those who would place the Church in the tribulation period. According to this passage two things must first happen before the Tribulation can possibly begin. Notice these two things which must precede the Tribulation, as they are given in verse 3. It states that "that day," the Day of the Lord, the Great Tribulation, shall not come "except there come a falling away first," and secondly, "that man of sin be revealed, the son of perdition." Notice carefully the two things which must first happen before the Tribulation can be inaugurated: they are (1) the Great Apostasy, or falling away, which is already here; and (2) the revelation of the man of sin, or the personal antichrist. Notice the words, *"that day"* – the Tribulation: ". . . that day shall not come, except there come a falling away first, and that man of sin be revealed, the son of perdition" (II Thessalonians 2:3).

The apostasy, the falling away, is already here, and so only one thing needs to be fulfilled before the Tribulation sets in and that is the revelation of the antichrist. But this man of sin, this antichrist, cannot be revealed until Someone else is first taken away out of the earth. There is Someone here in the world who prevents the antichrist from being revealed. But since the Tribulation cannot come until the antichrist is revealed, and he cannot be revealed until Someone now here is taken away, it follows naturally that everything waits for an event to remove the One who is holding back the man of sin. This event we shall see is the Translation of the Church away from the earth. With this in mind, I am sure that you will be able to understand the next verses,

> And now ye know what withholdeth that he [the antichrist] might be revealed in his time.
> For the mystery of iniquity doth already work [that is, preparation for the appearance of the antichrist is already in progress]: only he who now letteth [hinders] will let [hinder], until he be taken out of the way.
> And then shall that Wicked be revealed, whom the Lord shall consume with the spirit of his mouth . . . (II Thessalonians 2:6-8).

Here then we have the plain, unmistakable teaching of the Word of God. Follow the steps closely. First, the Tribulation or Day of the Lord cannot come until the antichrist is first revealed; second, this antichrist cannot come until He who now restrains and holds him back is first taken out of the way. Now who is this HE who holds back and restrains the coming of the antichrist and the bringing of the Great Tribulation? It *must* be a person, for He is called by the first personal pronoun, "until *he* be taken out of the way." Notice further that it is not only a person, but a supernatural person, one who is more powerful than Satan. Now what Person can restrain Satan? Certainly it must be someone more than a mere human; someone more powerful than the Devil himself, and this of course involves Deity. This *He* therefore, this restraining Person, must be a Person of the Trinity, and can only refer to the person of the Holy Spirit who, as we know, is in the world today indwelling and abiding in the Church and in every single believer.

This blessed person of the Holy Spirit is here now, abiding in the Church forever. He is the only One able to restrain Satan's man of sin from coming upon the earth. As long as this blessed Holy Spirit is personally here, the antichrist cannot be revealed. The words therefore are unmistakable, and we repeat again:

> For the mystery of iniquity doth already work: only he [the Holy Spirit] who now letteth [hinders] will let [restrain], until he be taken out of the way.
> And then shall that Wicked [man of sin] be revealed (II Thessalonians 2:7, 8).

As long, therefore, as the Holy Spirit is here the antichrist cannot come, and until he is revealed, the Tribulation cannot come; so it follows that until the Spirit is taken out in personal Pentecostal presence, the Tribulation cannot come. I do hope that I have made this clear and not wearied you by the repetition of this clear teaching. As long as the Church, indwelt by the Holy Spirit, is here upon the earth, the antichrist cannot come, and the Tribulation cannot set in.

This is the glorious truth that can give peace in the midst of the storm. We Christians often feel lonely and forgotten, for we receive but little recognition in this world if we follow the despised and ignored Nazarene Jesus. But we are, after all, the most important people in the world, so important that as long as we are here on the earth, the Devil himself cannot carry out his full program, and cannot produce the superman, the antichrist. Our presence in the world is the one thing which prevents the world's greatest tribulation and the crash of civilization. Yes, this is according to the Word of God. The thing which is today holding back the thunderstorm of world-wide conflagration and full-blast destruction is the presence in this world of a minority, a comparatively small body of born-again believers, indwelt by the Holy Spirit, who by their presence here are holding back Satan from putting his program into action. But once we are gone and He who now hinders is taken out of the way, great judgment will fall upon a Christ-rejecting world. Yes, we Christians are important people!

Jesus said, "Ye are the salt of the earth." Salt restrains and retards corruption, but it does not prevent ultimate corruption. It only retards it and holds it back for a time. So too the Church must be raptured before the Tribulation, just as surely as Noah had to be in the ark before the flood could come. Lot had to be out of Sodom before the fire could fall. This is the glorious blessed hope. What an assurance as we look about us at the gathering blackness of coming catastrophe, and hear the rumblings of imminent judgment. In the midst of a war-filled world, perplexed and plunging ever nearer to destruction, what a joy to hear Him say to us, "And when these things begin to come to pass, then look up, and lift your heads; for your redemption draweth nigh" (Luke 21:28).

Yes, indeed, one of these days it is really going to happen, for God Himself has said it. The Lord Himself shall descend from heaven with a shout, with the voice of the archangel, and with the trump of God, and the dead in Christ shall rise first. Then we which are alive and remain shall be caught up together with them in the clouds, to meet the Lord in the air, and so shall we ever be with the Lord. Is it any wonder that Paul concludes this passage on the blessed hope by the words, "Wherefore comfort one another with these words" (I Thessalonians 4:18)! The greatest comfort the Christian can find in these days of trouble and perplexity is the blessed hope that one of these days the Lord Jesus Christ Himself will return and set all things right. I declare, there is no hope in this world apart from the return of the One who made the world, and the only One who can straighten out its tangled skein. Man is indeed trying his best, but falls completely short, trying his best to bring peace with the limited means and powers which he has, but the Bible clearly states that there will be no lasting peace and blessing until the Prince of peace and blessing personally returns. In the gospel according to Luke, the disciples asked our Lord a very direct question while He sat upon Mount Olivet. It was: ". . . Master, but when shall these things be? and what sign will there be when these things shall come to pass?" (Luke 21:7).

What shall be the sign of Thy coming and the end of the world? Listen to the answer of Jesus:

> And there shall be signs in the sun, and in the moon, and in the stars; and upon the earth distress of nations, with perplexity; the sea and the waves roaring;
> Men's hearts failing them for fear, and for looking after those things which are coming on the earth: for the powers of heaven shall be shaken.
> And then shall they see the Son of man coming in a cloud with power and great glory.
> And when these things *begin* to come to pass, then look up, and lift up your heads; for your redemption draweth nigh (Luke 21:25-28).

Who can deny that these days are upon us? How important therefore the verses which follow:

> And take heed to yourselves, lest at any time your hearts be overcharged with surfeiting, and drunkenness, and cares of this life, and so that day come upon you unawares.
> Watch ye therefore, and pray always, that ye may be accounted worthy to escape all these things that shall come to pass, and to stand before the Son of man (Luke 21:34, 36).

Notice in this passage, very carefully, that Jesus declares that there will be a company who will escape all these things, referring to the tribulation period. Notice that these will escape *all* these things, referring to the Tribulation, not part, but *all*. One thing is clear. There will be a company when Jesus comes who will escape the horrors of the Tribulation.

Now the question arises: Who are these who shall escape all these things? According to First Corinthians there are only three classes of people in the world. We read: "Give none offence, neither to the *Jews*, nor to the *Gentiles*, nor to the *church* of God" (I Corinthians 10:32).

According to this Scripture there are only three classes of people in the world, called Jews, Gentiles, and the Church. According to the words of our Lord Jesus one of these groups will escape the trials of the Tribulation, and so the question is: Which group did Jesus have in mind? We know it cannot be Israel, for this will be the time of Jacob's trouble, and they will pass through it. We know also that it will not be the wicked Gentile nations, for this is their day of judgment. Only one class therefore remains, the Church of Jesus Christ. And so we repeat that verse again, "Watch ye, therefore, and pray always, that ye may be accounted worthy to escape all these things that shall come to pass, and to stand before the Son of man" (Luke 21:36).

It is therefore perfectly evident that the Church will not pass through the Tribulation, but escape all these things, and this is *that blessed hope.* This is the incentive for our pressing the battle, realizing that the Lord may come at any moment, and there is nothing that must still transpire before that event occurs. It is the greatest incentive in the world for holiness, for godliness, for evangelism, for soul winning, realizing that each day may be the last, and before the morning breaks we may stand before the Son of Man. This is the blessed hope of the dead in Christ, who eagerly await the day when their bodies too will be redeemed in the resurrection. This is our blessed hope that we shall see Him, and all the saints gone on before. And then, *perfection and eternity!*

Chapter Twenty-two

PEACE AT LAST

Nineteen hundred years ago our Lord taught His disciples to pray, "Thy kingdom come, Thy will be done, as in heaven, so in earth" (Luke 11:2). But although that prayer has not been answered as yet, we are nineteen hundred years nearer the time when it will be answered and when the heavenly voices will chant: "The kingdoms of this world are become the kingdoms of our Lord, and of his Christ; and he shall reign for ever and ever" (Revelation 11:15).

Time and space prevent us from mentioning the hundreds of passages in the Bible describing in glowing terms the glories of that golden age,

> When Christ shall have dominion
> Over land and sea;
> And earth's remotest regions
> Shall His empire be.

Of this glorious consummation Isaiah speaks:

> And it shall come to pass in the last days, that the mountain of the LORD's house shall be established in the top of the mountains, and shall be exalted above the hills; and all nations shall flow unto it.
>
> And many people shall go and say, Come ye, and let us go up to the mountain of the LORD, to the house of the God of Jacob; and he will teach us of his ways, and we will walk in his paths: for out of Zion shall go forth the law, and the word of the LORD from Jerusalem.
>
> And he shall judge among the nations, and shall rebuke many people: and they shall beat their swords into plowshares, and their spears into pruninghooks: nation shall not lift sword against nation, neither shall they learn war any more (Isaiah 2:2-4).

Can you imagine a time when war will be utterly unknown? Not a single armament plant will be operating, not a soldier or sailor will be in uniform, no military camps will exist, and not one cent will be spent for armaments of war, not a single penny will be used for defense, much less for offensive warfare. Can you imagine such an age, when all nations shall be at perfect peace, all the resources of earth available for enjoyment, all industry engaged in the manufacture of the articles of a peaceful state? Can you imagine a golden age when all the hospitals will be shut down, when all doctors and nurses will be out of a job, and medicines will be worthless and uncalled for? Can you imagine with me an age when there will be no poverty, when children will never die, when everyone will have everything he needs, and when violence and crime will be practically unknown? Can you imagine a time when there will be no wastelands, no storms, no droughts, no crop failures, no floods, and when even the wild animals will be tame and harmless, and will cease devouring one another?

I say again, Can you imagine such a coming golden age? Well, my friend, this is not merely imagination. It is a certain, unquestionable fact; as certain as the sun rises and sets. You ask me, Where in the world did you get that wild dream? Listen, my friend, it is not a wild dream, but the Word of the living God who made all the creation and the worlds. If you ask me where we find any such information, you have but to read your Bible, the Word of the Living God, for it is full of that glorious coming age of full redemption, and creation's restoration.

THE LAST DAYS

In the passage from Isaiah which we quoted at the beginning of this chapter, we are told when this glorious age will come. The prophet says: "And it shall come to pass in *the last days* . . ." (Isaiah 2:2).

Will you notice in this passage *two* things which are clearly set forth. First of all, the certainty of this event; and then the time of its fulfillment. God says, "It *shall* come to pass." *It shall come to pass.* Since it has never yet come to pass, and these conditions have never existed in this world, it must still lie in the future, for God Himself says, "it *shall* come to pass." Far be it from us to question the Word of the eternal God. And then will you notice the second thing. It will be in *the last days.* It will be at the close of the ages of man's sojourn upon this earth. These two things then, are absolutely definite.

Studying history, and looking upon the confused state of the world today, however, it does seem almost impossible that this could even be thought of. Think of it! After almost two thousand years of gospel preaching there are still more pagans and infidels in the world today than there have ever been before. After nineteen hundred years of preaching the Gospel of the Prince of Peace, this world has seen in a single genera- tion its two most devastating and cruel wars in all of its history, and today the fear of the third world war with its atomic horrors and consequences is gripping the entire world.

Crime is at an all-time high. Rumors and preparations for war fill the air and are plastered over all our newspapers. The Christian home has degenerated and the divorce evil has in- creased until it now approximates one divorce for every three marriages, sending an ever-increasing stream of neglected chil- dren from broken homes, into a cruel, unkind world, into a decaying society, to add to the already amazing volume of juvenile delinquency. Drunkenness is increasing by leaps and bounds. Moral standards are sinking lower and lower, while a jazz-crazy age is dancing its way into perdition in the very shadows of impending judgment.

HAS THE GOSPEL FAILED?

In the face of all these conditions, which no one can deny, we are led to ask, "Has the Gospel of the grace of God then failed?" Yes, Christianity is a colossal failure, and the Gospel of grace a farce and anything but the power of God, *if* we are to judge from the progress which we have made in converting the world in this present dispensation. But, beloved, Christianity is not a failure, and the Gospel is not a failure. Righteousness and truth and the Gospel will still prevail and triumph in the end, when the time comes for it in the long-range program of God. There is not a single verse in the entire Bible which teaches that it is God's plan that the whole world should be converted to Christ in this present dispensation. Quite to the contrary, the Bible teaches that wickedness will increase and become worse and worse until the very moment of Christ's Second Coming again. God's program for this age is not world conversion, but rather the taking out of a remnant of believers, a minority, to form the Body of Christ, and the Bride of our Lord, and when that number is full, according to God's sover- eign plan, then Jesus Christ will return, judge the nations of the earth, and then and then only the Kingdom will be set up, and world conversion result, when "every knee shall bow to him, and every tongue confess that Jesus Christ is Lord, to the glory of God the Father." This will be the time when the knowledge of the Lord shall cover the earth as the waters cover the sea, and when all men shall know Him, from the least even unto the greatest, and earth's golden age will then be ushered in.

GOD'S LONG-RANGE PROGRAM

If, therefore, it is God's program to convert the world, in this dispensation, then indeed, we repeat, God's program has utterly failed. But, beloved, it has not failed, because it is not God's program to convert the world before the coming of the Lord Jesus Christ. God's program is still running exactly on time and right on schedule. The golden age will come only when Jesus Christ returns to this earth, to catch away His Bride, then to judge and cleanse the earth, and then, *then*, after Jesus returns, will the hundreds of prophecies of earth's jubilee find their complete fulfillment.

AFFECTS ALL CREATION

This redemption of creation and restoration of that which Adam lost through sin will affect the entire earth, the people, the Nation of Israel, the animals, the plants, and even the soil. We shall point these out as we move along and study some of the glorious revelations of each one of these realms. But we want to direct your attention to the effect of Christ's return, first of all, on the Nation of Israel, for she is the central object of God's prophecy, and then upon the rest of the nations of the earth. The Old Testament prophecies are crowded with references to the final restoration of the Nation of Israel in the land of Palestine, but we would call your attention now to one which is representative of all the others:

> Behold, the days come, saith the LORD, that I will raise unto David a righteous Branch, and a King shall reign and prosper, and shall execute judgment and justice in the earth.
>
> In his days Judah shall be saved, and Israel shall dwell safely: and this is his name whereby he shall be called, THE LORD OUR RIGHTEOUSNESS.
>
> Therefore, behold, the days come, saith the LORD, that they shall no more say, The LORD liveth, which brought up the children of Israel out of the land of Egypt;
>
> But, The LORD liveth, which brought up and which led the seed of the house of Israel out of the north country,

and from all countries whither I had driven them; and they shall dwell in their own land (Jeremiah 23:5-8).

I am sure that you recognize that this has never yet been fulfilled, and that it therefore must still lie in the future. We believe with all of our heart that the return of the Nation of Israel politically to the land of Palestine in these recent years is the first step in the accomplishment of the full blessing of this passage, and many others in the Word of God. Judah and Israel shall dwell safely in the land of Palestine, never to be removed from it again. Not a single son of Jacob who survives the Great Tribulation, the day of Jacob's trouble, and belongs to the remnant of God's elect nation will be left or overlooked. The miraculous preservation of this miracle nation during all of these centuries and millenniums in the face of the most bitter odds, stands as a living testimony to the truth of the Word of God, that He will keep His covenant promise, and that He will keep every one of His assurances given to the house of Israel, from the days of Abraham, Isaac, and Jacob.

THE NATIONS BLESSED

Then, when Israel is back in the land, and Jesus Christ reigns upon the earth, then shall the promise of God come true which He made to Abraham when He said, "in thee shall all families of the earth be blessed" (Genesis 12:3). During the personal reign of the Lord Jesus wars will be unknown. There will be no battles, no navies, no armies, no arsenals, no ammunition plants, but all the ingenuity and inventive wisdom of men will be turned into useful production of implements of peace. Men will beat their swords into plowshares, and their spears into pruning-hooks. Peace and universal prosperity will abound, and "they shall not hurt nor destroy, saith the Lord, in all my holy mountain." There will be no poverty, nor unjust inequality. Sickness will be unknown, and death will be the rare exception, for the inhabitants shall not say, "I am sick." And even the soil shall be transformed by the presence of the King. Then will the words of Isaiah come true, which he uttered over twenty-five hundred years ago: "The wilderness and the solitary place shall be glad for them; and the desert shall rejoice, and blossom as the rose" (Isaiah 35:1).

The entire earth will be made productive again, and there will be no more deserts and bad lands, except Moab and Egypt, as reminders that even in this age of blessing God is still a just God.

DIVINE HEALING

This too will be the great age of future divine healing. Miracles and signs and healings belong to the Kingdom Age. That is why, when Jesus was here upon the earth offering the Kingdom· to Israel, it was the great age of signs and wonders and miracles. But they rejected the King, and the Kingdom was postponed, and now we live in the dispensation of faith, and not the dispensation of signs, for the —

> . . . Jews require a sign, and the Greeks seek after wisdom:
> But we preach Christ crucified. . . .
> . . . the power of God, and the wisdom of God (I Corinthians 1:22-24).

But when the Kingdom again is set up, and Israel is back in the land, all of these signs will characterize the presence of the King, and will return, for we read:

> Then the eyes of the blind shall be opened, and the ears of the deaf shall be unstopped.
> Then shall the lame man leap as an hart, and the tongue of the dumb sing: for in the wilderness shall waters break out, and streams in the desert (Isaiah 35:5, 6).

ANIMALS MADE TAME

Even the animal creation shall be changed and there shall be no more carnivorous beasts to waste and destroy and prey one upon the other. That will be the glad day spoken of by the prophets in describing this time of Christ's reign:

> The wolf also shall dwell with the lamb, and the leopard shall lie down with the kid; and the calf and the young lion and the fatling together; and a little child shall lead them.
> And the cow and the bear shall feed; their young ones shall lie down together: and the lion shall eat straw like the ox.
> And the sucking child shall play on the hole of the asp, and the weaned child shall put his hand on the cockatrice' den.
> They shall not hurt nor destroy in all my holy mountain: for the earth shall be full of the knowledge of the LORD, as the waters cover the sea (Isaiah 11:6-9).

Amid the violence and destruction of these days, can anyone assume that these glorious prophecies have ever been fulfilled?

Even though we try to spiritualize these prophecies, by no stretch of the imagination can we say that this has ever been true. The earth today is still filled with violence and destruction, and growing worse all the time. If the history of man is to be our guide, then there can only be one thing in the future — the utter destruction of man by his own wickedness and his own violence.

But God, who cannot lie, holds out a better hope than the gradual bringing in of the age of peace by man's feeble and fallible efforts. Instead, the Lord tells us that in the end time we shall hear of wars and rumors of wars, nation rising against nation, kingdom against kingdom, violence and destruction will increase, until He who said He would come will come. What a blessed thing to be able to look upon this world and all its conditions and see in them not the reason for despair and hopelessness, but the very signs of which Jesus said: ". . . when these things begin to come to pass, then look up, and lift up your heads; for your redemption draweth nigh" (Luke 21:28).

Chapter Twenty-three

EARTH'S GOLDEN AGE

The outline of prophecy culminates in the setting up of Christ's Millennial Kingdom at the end of the ages. It is the *Kingdom of Heaven upon* earth, when Heaven's King shall sit upon the Throne and the glorious millennial peace which the disciples expected at the Messiah's first coming, will be ushered in according to all the prophecies of the Bible. In these days of utter confusion among the nations it is indeed a glorious prospect which the Bible presents to us of that day when all the world will be united under one ruler and one King. We talk today about the "united nations" but it expresses only an ideal, a hope, a dream, rather than an accomplished fact. Man hopes for a united world at peace and does his utmost to achieve it, meeting only with failure again and again, but that dream will come true some day. It will not be brought about by human means or organization, but by the return of the Lord Jesus Christ to this earth. The city of Jerusalem will become the world capital, while all the earth is at peace. Hundreds of passages in Scripture deal with this golden age, many of which we have already referred to, but now we shall consider a number of others. First of all:

> And I will rejoice in Jerusalem, and joy in my people: and the voice of weeping shall be no more heard in her, nor the voice of crying.
> There shall be no more thence an infant of days, nor an old man that hath not filled his days: for the child shall die an hundred years old; but the sinner being an hundred years old shall be accursed.
> And they shall build houses, and inhabit them; and they shall plant vineyards, and eat the fruit of them.
> They shall not build, and another inhabit; they shall not plant, and another eat: for as the days of a tree are the days of my people, and mine elect shall long enjoy the work of their hands.
> They shall not labour in vain, nor bring forth for trouble;

for they are the seed of the blessed of the LORD, and their offspring with them (Isaiah 65:19-23).

This is an exceedingly rich passage of Scripture and we suggest that you study it for your own private devotion. There are several things to be noted which, as the context will clearly show, are a description of the conditions existing in this world during that coming golden age. The city of Jerusalem will be the world capital in that wonderful day when Jesus reigns upon the Throne of David.

First of all, will you notice that the Lord promises in this wonderful age, which we believe lies in the not-too-distant future, that sorrow and weeping and crying will be forever banished. The Lord will remove those things which are causing the sorrows of this world today. Satan, of course, during that age will be bound and cast into the bottomless pit. All men will at least nominally profess to know the Lord Jesus and bow the knee to Him, so that sorrow and troubles and trials which beset us today will be utterly unknown when Jesus reigns upon the Throne in Jerusalem. Then will you notice, in the second place, that this passage also teaches that life will be greatly prolonged during the millennial age. We read in this passage a very interesting account: "There shall be no more thence an infant of days, nor an old man that hath not filled his days: for the child shall die an hundred years old . . ." (Isaiah 65:20).

From this interesting passage we find that life will be so tremendously lengthened that a child will not mature until he is at least a hundred years old. All the processes of life will be slowed up, so that a child will remain a child for an entire century. As a result, since a child is not responsible until he has come to the years of accountability, and this age of accountability will not be reached in the Millennium until after a century of life here upon the earth, there can be no infant death of any kind. No one will die during the Millennium under one hundred years old, because the only cause of death will be open, deliberate, presumptuous rebellion against the King. The minimum span of life will be one hundred years, and only after the child has reached a hundred years, and the age of responsibility and accountability, will it be possible for it to die, and then, as we have stated, only in case of open rebellion against the King, the Lord Jesus. So that we read further;

". . . the sinner being an hundred years old shall be accursed" (Isaiah 65:20).

There will be no death, except violent death as a result of this open rebellion against the King of Kings. In the 22nd verse of this same chapter we read, "as the days of a tree are the days of my people, and mine elect shall long enjoy the work of their hands" (Isaiah 65:22).

Since a thousand years is with the Lord as one day, and one day is as a thousand years, we can understand these statements. You will recall that God said to Adam in the Garden, "The day thou eatest thereof thou shalt surely die." Since a thousand years is as one day with the Lord, God told Adam that he, because of sin, could not live out the span of one thousand years upon the earth, which is equal to one of God's days, and as a result Adam and all other antediluvians died before they ever reached the age of one thousand years. But at the coming of Christ and the setting up of the Kingdom, the curse will be removed, and then men will live out the full day of God, one thousand blessed years.

Sickness Will Be Unknown

We said a moment ago that the only death in the Millennium will be violent death, as a result of the immediate judgment of God upon open rebellion of sinners. We are further told in the Scriptures that sickness will be unknown during this blessed age of Christ's reign upon the earth. All sickness will be banished, for we read: "And the inhabitant shall not say, I am sick: the people that dwell therein shall be forgiven their iniquity" (Isaiah 33:24).

I realize that it is exceedingly difficult for us to imagine in this age of sorrow and sickness and suffering and death on every hand, that there could be a period of one thousand years when there will be no hospitals, no clinics, no ambulances screaming down our streets, for there will be no sickness and no disease. According to the Word of God, there will be only the occasional funeral service when someone has openly rebelled against the King of Kings and will therefore suffer the immediate judgment of Almighty God.

No More Poverty

The next thing we are told in this wonderful passage concerning the Millennium is that poverty and want shall be abolished forever and ever. Inequality among people will be wiped out, and there will be that common blessing of Almighty God upon all. We read once again: "And they shall build houses, and inhabit them; and they shall plant vineyards, and eat the fruit of them. They shall not build, and another inhabit; they shall not plant, and another eat . . ." (Isaiah 65:21, 22).

Everyone will be self-employed and will enjoy the full fruitage of his own labor. Micah in his prophecy tells us: "But they shall sit every man under his vine and under his fig tree . . ." (Micah 4:4).

Every single inhabitant of the world in that age will be independent, own his own property and his own home, and provide for his own family in abundance. There will be no want, there will be no hunger, there will be no thirsting, there will be no problem of distribution, there will be no famine of any kind, but all will have enough, and all will be satisfied.

The Bible tells us also that in this wonderful age, all of the religious controversy and strife and difference of opinion which has become such a reproach shall be forever ended. There will not be a large number of religions all contending one with another, but instead one great world religion will be the result. We read concerning the worship of this wonderful age:

> And many nations shall come, and say, Come, and let us go up to the mountain of the LORD, and to the house of the God of Jacob; and he will teach us of his ways, and we will walk in his paths: for the law shall go forth of Zion, and the word of the LORD from Jerusalem (Micah 4:2).

In this same vein we read the following:

> And they shall teach no more every man his neighbour, and every man his brother, saying, Know the LORD: for they shall all know me, from the least of them unto the greatest of them, saith the LORD: for I will forgive their iniquity, and I will remember their sin no more (Jeremiah 31:34).

And the Apostle Paul writing in the New Jerusalem also speaks of this coming day, when all of the divisions, not only of Christianity, but all religions will be forever past, and all men shall be worshipers of the Lord Jesus, at least in outward profession. Paul tells us that the day is coming when —

> . . . at the name of Jesus every knee should bow, of things in heaven, and things in earth, and things under the earth;
> And that every tongue should confess that Jesus Christ is Lord, to the glory of God the Father (Philippians 2:10, 11).

We have already touched upon the fact that during this age there will be universal peace. There will be no military training camps, no war planes, no battleships, no submarines, there will not even be any munitions factories, for in that day they shall "beat their swords into plowshares, and their spears into pruninghooks: nation shall not lift up sword against nation, neither shall they learn war any more." Time would utterly fail us to quote passage after passage from Scripture, all of them with one accord and without contradiction speaking of that glorious age for which every true child of God must be looking.

Truly, as we look upon conditions in the world today, if we did not have this hope of Christ's returning, and we had to rely upon the power of the Church, and the testimony of Christians to bring about the cessation of hostilities and to bring in perfect righteousness, I for one would despair and give up hope entirely. Personally, if I did not believe in the imminent, personal return of the Lord Jesus to make right that which is all wrong in this world today, and to bring in the peace for which man has so long been sighing, and for which he has so long been looking, I don't think I would care to preach another sermon. I would have to admit that the whole thing is a failure, and that the Gospel has not accomplished that which we had expected it to do, and that Christianity is nothing else but another religion and a tremendous farce.

But glory be to God, we have this assurance, we who know His program, that He who said He would come, will come, and will not tarry. His last promise which He left with His disciples was "I am coming again." The last promise of the Bible is: "He which testifieth these things saith, Surely I come quickly . . ." (Revelation 22:20).

And so we can praise God that in the midst of all the darkening shadows of impending judgment and the ominous shadows of dark days ahead, when men's hearts are failing them for fear of things which are coming to pass upon the earth, we can still believe for ourselves that everything is going to be all right, that God is still on the Throne, His program *is* being carried out in this world, and that soon He will come and take away the veil and explain all that which today remains so dark to us. But, we are not only happy that we can believe this for ourselves, and rejoice in the comfort which it brings to our own hearts, but we do thank God for the blessed privilege and opportunity of being able to bring it to others, this message of hope and cheer which the world so much needs today.

What a glorious, wonderful message it is to bring to a world which today is floundering about in dismay and confusion, not knowing whither to turn; and the darker the days become, the more glorious this blessed hope shines in our lives. I come with a message of encouragement, and hope, and assurance, and cheer, that one of these days, just as surely as Jesus came and died on the cross the first time, and arose from the grave, and ascended into Heaven, He is coming again; coming again to put a stop to all the wickedness and all the inequality and iniquity of this present day, put an end to man's rule of failure and bungling, and to set up His glorious, Millennial Kingdom. Yes, indeed, one of these days:

. . . the Lord himself shall descend from heaven with a shout, with the voice of the archangel, and with the trump of God: and the dead in Christ shall rise first:

Then we which are alive and remain shall be caught up together with them in the clouds, to meet the Lord in the air: and so shall we ever be with the Lord.

Wherefore comfort one another with these words (I Thessalonians 4:16-18).

Why say ye not a word of bringing back the King?
   Why speak ye not of Jesus and His reign?
Why tell ye of His kingdom, and of its glories sing,
   But nothing of His coming back again?

Dost thou not want to look upon His loving face?
   Dost thou not want to see Him glorified?
Would'st thou not hear His welcome, and in that very place,
   Where years ago we saw Him crucified?

O hark! creation's groans, How can they be assuaged?
   How can our bodies know redemptive joy?
How can the war be ended in which we are engaged,
   Until He come the lawless to destroy?

Come quickly, blessed Lord, Our hearts a welcome hold!
   We long to see creation's second birth;
The promise of Thy coming to some is growing cold,
   Oh, hasten Thy returning back to earth.

Bringing back the King, Oh, bringing back the King!
   The angel choirs of heav'n their hallelujahs sing;
Bringing back the King, Oh, bringing back the King!
   Ye ransomed, let your joyous welcome ring!

EVEN SO, COME, LORD JESUS!